LANCE A A
You ARE A
Good Man and A
Good Friend. Your World
Family means The will Also
To Me and I
Cherish The and I Hope
your Book Good Times.
The Buddy and Bless!
God
Ronnie
Coach -
JEREMIAH 28:11

The Life Coach

The Life Coach

Small-Town Lessons on Faith, Family, and Football

Ronnie Gage, M.Ed. and
Emmet C. (Tom) Thompson II, D.S.L.

with Alice Sullivan

Clovercroft Publishing

The Life Coach

Published by Clovercroft Publishing, Franklin, Tennessee

Scripture is used from the New King James Version, © 1982 by Thomas Nelson, Inc.
All rights reserved. Used by permission.

Edited by Adept Content Solutions

Cover Design by Rachel Thompson

Interior Design by Suzanne Lawing

Printed in the United States of America

978-1-948484-93-0

Ronnie and I have been close friends for forty years. Over the years, I have witnessed him strive to be a mentor to other coaches and a positive role model for his players. He has faced many different experiences in his life, from devastating personal loss to the ultimate success in the coaching profession. No matter how difficult the situation, Ronnie has always demonstrated a strong faith in God, a deep love for family and friends, and a passion for the sport of football. You will find many of the experiences that he writes about to be uplifting, enlightening, and entertaining.

—TERRY GOODE, FORMER DEFENSIVE
COORDINATOR AND BEST FRIEND

I could tell Ronnie Gage was an extraordinary man the first time I met him and he shared some of his life story—his triumphs and his sorrow. He has the heart of a champion, is an amazing husband and father, and has a passion for football, family and faith. The football field was his classroom, and he motivated young men every day to reach their full potential. He made a positive impact in my life, and I am confident this book will provide great advice and guidance for all who read his message.

—BARBARA PONDER, ASSISTANT SUPERINTENDENT
OF PERSONNEL, BARBERS HILL ISD

I was fortunate to have served as deputy superintendent for the Lewisville Independent School District in Texas for twenty-four years. During that time, Ronnie Gage served as the head football coach at Lewisville High School and later as the district's athletic director.

During Ronnie's tenure as head football coach, he led his teams to two Texas 5A State Football Championships, earning his place in the Texas High School Coaches Association Hall of Fame.

Coach Gage stands out in my mind for far more that the multiple district and state championships that were achieved under his leadership. He was a builder of character for hundreds of young men and was a mentor for countless coaches. Ronnie genuinely cared for, no loved his players, and they loved him. Yes, he taught them about winning football games, but more importantly, Coach Gage taught them about life and how to live it the right way. He modeled honor, sportsmanship, respect, and character for his players and coaches. From him they learned about loyalty, the value of hard work, goal setting, commitment, and teamwork.

Ronnie Gage modeled two even more important qualities for his players and staff members in my eyes. He taught them the importance of family and Christian values. They learned how to be young men who would win at life.

Finally, I once told Coach Gage that I wish that my own son had had the opportunity to play for him.

—**MICHAEL G. KILLIAN, PhD**
(LEWISVILLE ISD DEPUTY SUPERINTENDENT, RETIRED)

How do you condense down to a quote, what someone who has had such a tremendous impact on me and my family means to me?

I sat in the fieldhouse as the football booster club meeting was about to start, worrying that I would be dismissed as "one of those parents" who saw something in their child that no one else did. See my son, Justin Cade, is autistic and wanted to play football for a coach who had two state championships under his belt.

Ronnie Gage welcomed Justin as part of the team. He helped to mold my son and fostered a lifelong way of being:

You can do "it" with hard work, determination, honor and integrity. Whatever the "it" is.

Regardless of the odds, with God, family and community, there is nothing that can stop you but you.

I do not look at Ronnie Gage as a head football coach or athletic director. I look at Ronnie Gage as a "maker of men."

—**RONNI CADE**, BOOSTER CLUB PRESIDENT 2000-05,
MOTHER OF PLAYER, AND FRIEND

What a privilege it has been for me to be a part of the coaching staff of Ronnie Gage. My seven years working with Ronnie at Lewisville were life changing indeed. I met a man that loved his family and chose to incorporate them as a huge part of his football program.

Ronnie is a man's man who teaches the grind and works the players hard and believes in establishing a mentality of extreme toughness. At the same time, he told the kids daily that he loved them and wanted the best for them. The players adored and loved him because they knew how much he cared. With the coaches, it was the same. He loved us and mentored us by giving us the freedom to coach. When I became a head coach, I modeled the way I did things after him and his philosophy: Coach the little things, love the players as people, and make sure you include your family in your profession.

Ronnie is a very competitive person who got the best out of us all (players and coaches). Because Ronnie believed in me, he gave me the opportunity to be a head coach and paved the way for me to serve in the Texas High School Coaches Association. Ronnie makes people better than they thought they could be. An incredible gift.

Finally, Ronnie is a man of faith and was never bashful about his faith in Christ. Faith, family, and football is Ronnie Gage. He is a hall-of-fame coach and a man with more awards than can be counted. But what means the most to Ronnie is the continued relationships with his past players and coaches, and we all cherish his wisdom and the time we spent with him. Great man!

—**BRIAN BRAZIL**, LEWISVILLE HS COACH, 1992–98;
HEBRON HS HEAD COACH, 1999–PRESENT

This story is about one of the best high school coaches in Texas high school football history. This is a book from the heart about a coach's passion to coach kids while keeping family and faith in the forefront. A great book written by a great coach!

—**JOE MARTIN**, EXECUTIVE DIRECTOR,
TEXAS HIGH SCHOOL COACHES ASSOCIATION

Dedicated to Jessica Gage Bonesio

"Charm is deceitful and beauty is passing,
But a woman who fears the Lord, she shall be praised.
Give her of the fruit of her hands,
And let her own works praise her in the gates."
—Proverbs 31:30–31, NKJV

"God, whether I get anything else done today, I want to make sure that I spend time loving You and loving other people—because that's what life is all about. I don't want to waste this day."
—Jessica Gage Bonesio

"My relationships with people are what prepare me for eternal life, and nothing else will matter when I face God. I will pray that my relationships, not just my close relationships, but all, will always take priority over every other thing in my life. Loving is the most important thing: not work, school, or gain. Character is my legacy."
—Jessica Gage Bonesio

Acknowledgments from Coach Ronnie Gage

Coaching is all about people who love and care about each other. It is about hard work and support. It is about trust and believing in each other. It is about respect and loyalty. It is about competing at a high level.

Throughout my career, I have been surrounded by the best! We truly cared about each other and we had fun. The success I have experienced is a direct result of the many coaches, friends, and family who have been the foundation. It was built on a system and it worked because of the love, professionalism, and hard work of so many.

To my wife, Stephanie, who is the love of my life, my inspiration, and my best friend.

Jess, Juli, and James who have made me proud to be a father.

Sean and Lindsey for embracing our family and the lifestyle that came with it.

Crew, Millie, and Maeva for always making "Coach" smile.

Karen, Kathy, and Robert for supporting my dream.

My mom for raising four of us by herself and giving me the opportunity to chase a dream.

Terry Goode, Gary Prescott, Bill Pietrosky, and Alan Perrin for the good times, fun times, and having my back during tough times.

The many other coaches and teachers who always made me better because of their commitment to excellence.

The players who always gave me their best and did not let the fear of failure come into play.

Tom for his friendship and his motivation to pursue new directions.

Alice who made this book a reality.

A loving God who has given me all that I have.

"I can do all things through Christ who strengthens me."
(PHILIPPIANS 4:13)

—RONNIE GAGE

Acknowledgments from
Emmet C. (Tom) Thompson II

In writing *The Life Coach*, I would like to thank my wife, Teresa, for her love and support. In addition, I would like to thank my coauthor, Coach Ronnie Gage, for his friendship and for believing in me to make the kick of a lifetime. As well, I want to offer a heartfelt thank-you to Alice Sullivan for her phenomenal way of turning words into a book. In addition, I want to express my appreciation to Larry Carpenter and my daughter, Rachel Thompson, for their above-and-beyond support.

Finally, I would like to thank the many individuals who have supported this project and had a special impact on my life, including Keith Yates, Dr. Tedd Mitchell, Dr. Kenneth H. Cooper, Dr. Bruce Winston, Dr. Charles Manz, Dr. Christopher P. Neck, Dr. Bob Peters, Tony Kaufman, John Anderson, Shane Hazelwood, Joe Fernandez, Glenn Gottlich, Ed Daves, Larry Rudisill Sr., David Norman, Loren Dawson, Tim Millerick, Lynn McCain, Benita Teems, Danya Clairmont, Shad Teems and many other colleagues and friends too numerous to name here.

On a personal note…I would like to say thank-you to Dr. Peter J. Daniels for his friendship, wisdom, and encouragement. My own destiny, as well as the destiny of my family, has been and continues to be influenced by him. Furthermore, to me our friendship is a life treasure. I will never forget his timely words of encouragement, "God rewards faithfulness." Those words continue to guide my daily life.

—Dr. Emmet C. (Tom) Thompson II

Foreword

Coaching is one of the greatest professions in the world for the simple fact that coaches can be some of the most influential people in our entire society. If you think about it, coaches have been given the unique opportunity to work closely with hundreds of young people on almost a daily basis to develop not only knowledge and physical skills, but worthy values, attitudes, and character traits. I am excited about Ronnie Gage's book *The Life Coach* because Ronnie focuses on these things, and it is these intangibles that are most important to the coaching profession.

Over the years that Ronnie Gage and I have known each other, it seems every time we got together, we would talk about what it takes to be a "successful coach." Something we always agreed on was that we should use our position of leadership to coach and teach "beyond the game." Ronnie lives his life in such a way and coached in such a way that he was a role model for his players. There are times he was the dad that some players never had. Having strong role models is a must for our society. Role modeling is an essential part of teaching values and developing positive character traits.

Ronnie Gage is not only a successful high school coach, he is an outstanding husband and father and teacher. Ronnie Gage is one of Texas high school football's most committed and dedicated coaches. He is a man of principle and has lived his life in complete harmony with his values. Coach Gage coaches for the right reasons—to change lives through his influential power as a coach.

What excites me about Coach Gage's book is that it can help each of us do our jobs better and more effectively. *The Life Coach* is a must read for every aspiring coach and those who would simply like to improve their purpose and passion for coaching.

—D.W. RUTLEDGE
FORMER EXECUTIVE DIRECTOR,
TEXAS HIGH SCHOOL COACHES ASSOCIATION

Contents

Family Dynamics and My Parents' Marriage
Parents' Involvement and Roles
The Relationship with My Father
My Father's Illness
Huddle Up with Tom Thompson: For the Love of the Game
Driven by Anger
Developing Self-Leadership

Coaches Who Stepped In
The Power of Mentorship
Huddle Up with Tom Thompson: When Life Is Your Mentor
Choosing Family over Football
Fumbling through Life
God Is the Ultimate Coach

Meeting Stephanie
Encouraging Each Other and Making It Work
Deciding to Become a Coach
Landing My Dream Job
Becoming a Father

The Unlikely Friendship Formed on and off the Field

Let's face it, the "game of life" consists of good, bad, and ugly events. To top it off, *this game* of life is competitive, very competitive—maybe even more so than Texas football, if you can believe it. If you've ever run suicides in 100-degree weather in full uniform, you know how hard it is to compete at a high level during practices. That same level of competition and drive is required to win games and titles. That same determination is required to have any measure of success in life, as coaches Ronnie Gage and Tom Thompson can attest to.

Still, God makes things happen in the most unexpected ways.

Who would have thought that an ambitious first-time college coach—Ronnie Gage—and a determined 61-year-old man—Tom Thompson—would be brought together to discuss Tom's eligibility and a chance to play college football? The end results were a partnership in which one man was able to achieve his dream and the other helped him make it happen. They developed a life-long friendship, which includes mutual respect and love. God definitely had a hand in making this happen.

Throughout *The Life Coach,* you'll learn the humble beginnings behind one of Texas high school football's most successful coaches. As Ronnie Gage takes us back to where his love of football first began, he shares his greatest joys as well as his greatest losses. But through it all, he's been blessed to have a strong and supportive family and football community.

At the end of each chapter, in a section entitled "Huddle Up with Tom Thompson," Tom shares applicable life lessons, anecdotes, and a surprisingly unique (and often parallel) view of faith, family, and football, having a positive attitude, and keeping life events in perspective. You'll also discover the unlikely friendship that was forged on the field between these two men, which flourished because of their mutual respect of the game.

The Life Coach will challenge the reader to not take the little things in life for granted, as both men share valuable winning life lessons that offer an individual the opportunity to develop a successful game plan, or playbook. More importantly, Coach Ronnie Gage's example of being a champion, both on and off the field, will inspire the reader to win at the "game of life."

Both men know that with God, all things are possible.

With hard work, and supportive friends and family, you can achieve any goal you put your mind to.

And when it comes to football in Texas, when all those factors are in play on the field—and in one's life—miracles can happen.

Coach Ronnie Gage and Emmet C. (Tom) Thompson II, Austin College Roos, 2009–10

1

Humble Beginnings in Decatur, Texas

I'm on the back side of time now, but the Decatur, Texas, I grew up in wasn't a place anyone would bat an eyelash at. The population has doubled to 6,000 souls since my youth, but some things never change. Everyone in Decatur knows everyone and knows what you're having for dinner before the first plate hits the table. You'd be "going to town" if you made the forty-five-minute drive into Dallas, and you'd be missed if you didn't tell anyone you were going. All the things you'd expect out of a small American town existed in Decatur, and I wouldn't have wanted to grow up anywhere else.

Of all the time-honored traditions that cling to Decatur, the desire to play high school football and become a Decatur Eagle hooked me from an early age. I remember everything about the Friday night football games. The smell of cut grass. Streamers flapping on the goal posts. The band playing our fight song. The lights buzzing and attracting moths. Then there were the players. I thought the boys who wore an Eagle's jersey were heroes. And I wasn't the only one. The Eagles were as an important part of life in Decatur as church on Sunday. The game and its players were bigger than life, and I wanted to be a part of it.

1970, Ronnie's senior year as a Decatur Eagle

1970, Senior year, Stephanie cheers for Decatur Eagles

In those days, they didn't have a lot of the pee-wee, early age competitive sports we see now. My friends and I never knew it, but we had a good background for competitive sports before we ever stepped onto a field. Back then, there was a natural rhythm to life as a young boy. You got home from school, did your chores, got on your bicycle, and hung around the ballfields. That's just the way it had always been, and there were endless opportunities for boys in Decatur to be around, and involved in, athletics.

Since there weren't any youth football or basketball leagues back then, you had to wait until you were in the seventh grade—so twelve or thirteen years old—to try your hand at any organized sport, but I had always been a "fieldhouse junkie" and that might have given me a small advantage. I was the kid who stayed around until the coaches and referees were ready to leave and lock the gates. Every chance I had, I was in the coach's office, cutting up and talking to the adults like I was one of them. In the presence of my elders, I was like a human sponge with shaggy hair and a bright smile. I focused on everything they said, from discussing plays to fieldhouse stories. I knew if I wanted to play, I had to work exceptionally hard. I wasn't a great athlete by any means, but I was very competitive and able to find my way, with the help of the coaches.

With hard work and strategy, I made the cut whenever I tried out for any team. I was an all-district basketball player, ran track, was a twelve-foot pole-vaulter, and slugged a baseball outside of school. Still my favorite was football, and I was determined to make the high school team.

All that hard work eventually produced a 150-pound center and safety for the Eagles. Getting my blue and white number fifty jersey was one of the proudest days of my life, but I also was observant enough to know my time as a football player would be relatively short-lived. Even as a teenager, I knew there wasn't going to be any demand for someone of my size and talent level from Decatur, Texas, of all places. There would not be a long line of college recruiters trying to win me over, and no pro football in my future. But what I did know by high school was that sports had been an important enough outlet in my life that I didn't want it to end after high school.

I realized early on that even if I wasn't playing on the field, I could do what every one of those coaches did for me. I could patiently watch and listen to a young person and guide them on how to be a better athlete. From some of the troubles my family had gone through, I learned how to navigate tough times. There's something about adversity that brings out the best or worst in people. Thankfully, with the support of my family and coaches, I chose to let the hard times bring out the best in me. I wanted to take those hard-won lessons to help others bring out the best version of themselves—on and off the playing field. I knew then that I wanted to be a coach.

Family Dynamics and My Parents' Marriage

The first team any person belongs to is their family. I am the second child of four siblings. My older sister, Karen, is two years older than I am. She's the family musician and can play anything you put in front of her on the piano. My youngest sister, Kathy, is three years younger than me and played college basketball. My brother Robert is five years younger than I am and was a three-sport athlete like myself. I say that we were a team because we had to depend on each other during our family's stormy times.

Our parents absolutely adored me and my siblings, but they didn't always get along. When I was younger, my parents' relationship was often volatile and unpredictable, rocky to say the least. I didn't know it at the time, but I think he had a little bit of a drinking problem. He hid it well from us, but when I think back on things, I'm sure that played a part in some of their arguments and difficulties. The good news was that over the years, my parents were able to work out their differences.

Although they never got a divorce, they lived separate a lot, and I'm sure that helped ease the tension. My brother and I lived with my dad and the two girls lived with my mom for a while. We were shuttled between the two homes quite a bit during that time, and the strain was apparent on us as kids as well as my parents. One day we might think Mom was being too hard on us, and the next day it might be Dad. What made our situation tough was that even though the adults were fighting with each other, they each loved their children to death, which meant we often felt like we were caught in the middle, and we tried not to pick sides. As kids often do, we dealt with the emotional turbulence just like you would with an unexpected rainstorm. You take shelter where you can and try not to get wet.

Parents' Involvement and Roles

Even with my parents being frequently at odds with each other, it didn't keep them from supporting their children's endeavors, so that was a blessing. My mother was the true hero when it came to supporting our activities and interests. Even though my mom had chronic asthma, neither my siblings nor I remember her ever missing a single game or school function we were involved in—and that's saying a lot since we were all fairly active kids.

Since cold weather was one trigger for her asthma attacks, she wasn't able to sit outside in the cold and watch me play football, so my mother got creative. In order to watch my football games, Mom found more ways to get inside stadiums with her car than anyone I've ever known. She sat in her warm car to watch the game, with no chance of the weather triggering an attack, and with comfortable seating too. Indoor sports were a lot easier on her health, and every basketball game I ever played in, there was Mom sitting on the hard-wooden bleachers, cheering me on and offering the referees advice.

Possibly the biggest gift Mom gave me was that she never interfered in anything I did. She wasn't one of those parents who hovered and made sure everything worked out in our favor. My path and the paths of my siblings were for us to find our own way, to succeed and to fail, and to gain confidence from trying again. We were free to pursue our own hobbies and passions without pressure, and Mom would always cheer us on. Of course, that support came with the price of not giving us a lot of sympathy if things didn't go the way we wanted. If I was going to play a sport, I was expected to give it my best, not to come home whining. If it didn't work out, then it didn't work out. We stood or fell on our own merits, and that taught us a lot about building character and taking responsibility for our actions and decisions.

That's not to say my mother didn't have a kind heart. At Christmas and Thanksgiving, Mom worked double duty to make sure everyone was fed and happy. She not only fixed meals for our family, but she fixed food for just about every neighbor we had. There were several elderly people who lived nearby, and she always made sure they had something on the table for the holidays.

For many years, Mom worked in Decatur's welfare department. At Christmas time, she gathered presents and made sure the less fortunate kids had a good Christmas. Back then, I didn't give her actions much thought. It was simply something she did every year. Now, I realize how important those acts of kindness were and that she didn't have to give back to the community—she chose to because she knew it was important. We all have a duty to our communities that goes beyond taking care of our own. That's one of the best coaching lessons I took from Mom.

The Relationship with My Father

1982, Young Coach Gage gets to meet the legend, Bear Bryant.

My relationship with my father didn't have time to develop in the same ways as it did with my mother. Dad was a blue-collar worker who drove thirty-five miles to work. Every day he'd hit the road with his sack lunch, give his eight hours, and come home to his kids. He was in his early forties when I was born but still found time to teach me baseball. He played on summer leagues back in his day and passed down everything he knew to me as he coached my Little League team. That was the greatest hallmark of my dad's life—his kids came first. No matter how tired he was from working or a long drive, my dad always had time for us.

If I learned how to be supportive and how to take care of others from my mother, I learned how to be persistent and flexible from my father. Dad never made a lot of money, but he was there every day to make sure we had what we needed. That included the times when he and Mom weren't together.

Dad did household roles that, back in those days, were reserved for women. That didn't matter to my father, because he had the duty to care for his children. That never stopped, and he would adapt however he needed to take care of us. Until he got sick.

My Father's Illness

There was a spot on Dad's hand that wouldn't go away. I never saw the actual lesion because it was stained red from the Mercurochrome Dad kept dabbing on it. The mercury-laced antiseptic was a cure-all back in my day. Except Mercurochrome couldn't heal what Dad had. When the wound didn't heal on its own, Dad finally went to the doctor. I remember being at my grandmother's house when Dad got back from his appointment. There wasn't any way of sugar-coating the news his doctor thought it was cancer.

As a thirteen-year-old boy, I didn't know much about cancer. I just knew Dad said lesions that don't heal on their own are an indication of some types of cancer. That sore spot on Dad's hand landed him with a diagnosis of lung cancer. He had been a heavy smoker, a combat veteran, and laborer after the war. Looking back, there's no telling what all ended up in my father's lungs aside from cigarette smoke over the years. It makes sense now why my father contracted the deadly disease, but as a thirteen-year-old boy, the world made no sense.

Dad started receiving treatments at Harris Hospital forty miles away from Decatur. We drove back and forth from Harris so much that summer; I don't exactly remember what the schedule was or how often Dad had to go. It seemed that we were always tired and on the road to or from the hospital. The stress of a sick loved one wears a family's nerves slick.

Mom had been used to periods when she took care of everything on her own when she and Dad had their short separations, but this was different. Suddenly she had to shoulder a weight no spouse should ever have to—becoming a widow with four kids if her husband died. Even though she didn't *like him* most days, she still loved him and hated to see him in pain.

After each treatment, we always thought Dad was going to be okay. He was a little better today, wasn't he? We looked for any sign that his health was improving, and some days, it seemed like he was on the mend. Of course, as a kid, there's always an abundance of optimism until the truth is so overwhelming that you can't imagine a rosy outlook anymore.

Slowly, the days turned into an ever-thinning downhill line. They put Dad in the hospital for around forty days as his outlook and his color grew more and more dim. I stayed with Dad as much as I could and tried not to think about it too much. I didn't really understand what death was, but I knew things would be different, scary, and unknown. I just wanted my dad back, moody disposition and all.

There was a couch in the hospital I claimed as my bed for the nights I stayed. Mom was there as much as she could be, but she had to work even harder now to take care of everyone, and she still had my younger siblings to care for on her own. Life had to go on for the rest of us, even as my father lay dying, so we all pitched in, helping where we could. We quickly learned how to be responsible, and our mother sacrificed time and money to make sure we had the essentials.

And then one day, he was gone.

You don't ever really understand finality until it happens.

After he died, I don't remember grieving a lot. I think when you've gone through the ordeal of watching somebody suffer as much as he did, there is a little bit of relief that accompanies death. At least he wasn't suffering anymore.

There was certainly a sadness, but that part of my father's passing is mostly lost to time. I do know there were those who lovingly patted me on the back and reminded me I "was the man of the house now." Thankfully, I didn't feel that there was an official burden on my shoulders like that at home. But I knew there were things I was going to have to do to keep the house running as smoothly as possible. We all did what was necessary and expected of us. I'm sure I learned that lesson from my mother. And as it turns out, the time we lived with our father helped in the long run because we all knew how to wash clothes, do chores, and cook. That came in handy when Mom became a single parent.

Her reaction to my father's death was to grieve in private. Whatever differences there were between her and my dad had been worked out before he went, so at least she held no residual anger toward him. Mom coped by throwing herself into the work of a single mother of four. There was always some activity she was involved in to tamp down the loss. There were never-ending lunches to pack, laundry to fold, or a job to work that diffused her suffering.

HUDDLE UP WITH TOM THOMPSON:
FOR THE LOVE OF THE GAME

My father loved to watch football on TV. When I think about my father and football, one game comes to mind. It was a Texas versus California game in 1959, and I was eleven years old. I don't even remember the Texas whos or the California whats. All I know is that my dad liked to watch football and we both loved how Texas played.

Football mattered to me because it mattered to my father. Football also mattered to me because it was the game of choice in my neighborhood. If I was going to have any interaction with the neighborhood boys, it was going to be while playing football. Now, I was not a very good neighborhood football player. At best, I was a second-tier pick on a neighborhood team, but I enjoyed playing, and my enthusiasm often made up for my lack of talent.

My parents didn't have a great marriage, and my father left home when I was in the sixth grade. I missed him terribly because a young boy craves his father's presence and guidance. It also meant I wouldn't be able to watch Texas on that black-and-white TV with him anymore. The games of catch in the front yard would have to be with borrowed dads. The guy across the street had played football at SMU, and sometimes he'd throw the ball with me. He was the first person to show me how to punt a football, a skill that would come in handy decades later. I made the best of my family situation, and even though I went to live with him during my sophomore year of high school, there was a gap in my life where my father should have been and an anger brewing under the surface.

I didn't get good enough in football to be noticed by anyone until I was a junior in high school. Until then, I had clocked all of five minutes of game time my freshman year, but it wasn't necessarily because I wasn't a decent player. I couldn't participate most of the time because of my lousy grades. My school district didn't let anyone play any sport if they were failing a class. I was usually on academic probation one semester and off it by the next. Unfortunately, my bad semester was usually during football season. Track season came with better grades, so I lettered in track because it was the only sport I was ever truly eligible for, even though I loved football much more.

Driven by Anger

Growing up in a single-parent home with a less-than-loving mother, I wasted a lot of time during my teenage years being angry. My home life had been fractured. Unlike Coach Gage's situation, where his father's untimely departure made the family pull together and become stronger, when my father left, it only gave my mother another thing to complain about. That I always reminded her of her *deadbeat ex-husband* didn't help, and she verbalized that often, leaving me feeling worse than chopped liver. My situation remained that way until the summer of 1966, when my mother was so tired of seeing me that she threw me out of the house to live with my dad. Then I asked my dad to send me to military school because I was craving structure. After he agreed, I moved in with my aunt and uncle in Florida.

Only one constant remained: the football field, which was my therapy. When I was on the football field, I took out all my anger. Running down field, tackling, dodging, whatever I was doing, there was anger seeping out of my pores like black sweat. I couldn't possibly see what my tribulations would yield us down the road. Instead, I focused on the pain and let it become my driving force for the foreseeable future.

But of course, good seeds were being planted all along the way, even if I was too blind (or angry or stubborn) to notice. Even though my dad loved football, I don't know if he could have taught me how to kick. If I hadn't learned how to kick, thanks in part to my SMU neighbor, I wouldn't have scored in an NCAA football game at the age of sixty-one. How could I have known as a heartbroken young man that act of kindness would lead me to becoming a record holding football player—*in my sixties?* We must see every obstacle as an opportunity, keep an open mind, be vigilant, and pray a lot.

Developing Self-Leadership

Both Ronnie and I lost the guidance of our fathers at about the same time in our lives. Even though we each would have mentors and wildly different paths before we met each other, we both were forming the basis of self-leadership. If you're unfamiliar with the concept, self-leadership is influencing yourself to achieve your goals. It's holding yourself accountable when no one else will. It's finding a way when there's no one else to give you guidance. It's understanding that tough times are preparing you for greater things.

The term self-leadership probably didn't exist when Ronnie and I were kids. We both understood the concept of guiding ourselves, but the takeaway is that in our lives, we're not in competition with anyone but ourselves.

It would be easy for me to think that I was a failure because I didn't achieve X by Y time just because someone else did that. But that would be a mistake, because placing limitations on ourselves, especially by comparison to others, is a sure way to keep ourselves from achieving our goals. When we push the boundaries of what is possible for us, then we become winners.

Looking to someone else for inspiration or as a mentor, instead of for purposes of comparison—now that's the right track for personal growth. We lose when we get disheartened because a goal comes easier or more quickly for someone else. We also lose out when we place more emphasis on the accolades and acceptance of others. Where your dreams and goals are concerned, look within and to the Lord for validation and encouragement. You were made to achieve great things. And great things take time and practice!

As I mentioned in my book *Get a Kick Out of Life,* few of us are born, or wake up on a random Tuesday morning, with a clear perception of our own abilities. Self-efficacy—the cross point where an idea meets the confidence to act—is learned, just like other tools such as self-motivation, optimism, and perseverance. We learn self-efficacy by breaking down goals into smaller attainable increments that we can work toward daily, and those successes give us confidence in our abilities.

As painful as they are at the time, the beginnings of heartbreak and setbacks can be defining moments if you allow them to be. And they can happen at any point in our lives, whether six or sixty. Life is constantly changing, and when we understand that we are the authors of how that change plays out, then we can truly enjoy our new beginnings.

2

Mentors Who Made a Difference

A good coach doesn't see an athlete as just a player on the court or field. What goes on in a young person's life outside of practice and games is as important, or more so, than what happens when they suit up. If a young person's parents or caregivers don't have the financial or emotional means to cover a child's basic needs, their performance will suffer in all areas—athletic, educational, social, and emotional.

1993, Two of Ronnie's mentors, Neal Wilson, athletic director, and Doug Killough, principal.

Sometimes all it takes is a coach or teacher to step up and invest a little extra time in and attention to those kids who appear to be suffering. Even a small gesture can go a long way. And you never know . . . it could even change the trajectory of their entire lives. Coaching is about people who love and care about each other. It is about hard work and support. It is about trust and believing in each other. Most of all, it is about respect and loyalty. I have been surrounded by the best in the business ever since my youth, and there are a couple of coaches who came into my life at just the right time.

Coaches Who Stepped In

Coach Neal Wilson came to Decatur my eighth-grade year, and he coached me all the way through high school. My father had died in the spring of my seventh-grade year, so Coach Wilson wasn't there when my father passed away, but he knew my situation. We never had a one-on-one talk about my father. From my perspective, Coach Wilson "just knew" and tried to play a part in my development as a young man. He was the strongest male influence I had in my life, and he was responsible for helping me realize my potential.

A couple of years later, Bob Bogue came into my life as my basketball coach and the assistant football coach. He worked closely with Coach Wilson, and they were two of the most influential figures in my life. In fact, these men had a sense of guidance I've always patterned my coaching after.

Coaches Wilson and Bogue saw the void my father's death left in my life. They offered love and acceptance, something every young boy needs. They didn't treat me any differently and held me to the same standards and expectations as the rest of the team, and honestly, that made a big difference. They didn't coddle me or slack up on pushing me the same way they did with the other players. They just took a little more interest in my off-the-field life than some of their other athletes. Coach Bogue, for example, worked closely with Mom to give us kids some direction as far as going to college. He was always there in any way he could be. He was a great motivator and always gave me encouragement to work harder and get better. He helped me to see the end result of hard work.

The kind of coaching I received from Coach Wilson and Coach Bogue can't be faked, and their example has helped me as an educator and a coach when dealing with kids who are experiencing tough times.

I'd go on to work for Coach Wilson when I got out of college. He's since passed away, but even after he retired, there wasn't a week that passed when we didn't talk. I had a relationship with Coach Wilson for forty-three years, and I always felt like I could get fatherly advice as well as professional advice when needed.

1993, The Thrill of Victory after the 1993 State Championship win.

Coach Bogue has retired to Colorado now, yet I still stay in touch to see how he's doing. Those types of life-long bonds don't spring up when you don't care or do the minimum at your job. I know to this day that they both cared for me. And I have been blessed to have such men of integrity in my life.

The Power of Mentorship

Unlocking the power of mentorship rests in balancing the help you give with high expectations. I can be sympathetic when an athlete has grown up in a bad situation. I've gone through those tough times, but I lived through it. The key still comes down to common sense, decision-making, and knowing what you want to do with your life. You can only ride the crutch of "my life has been horrible" so far. There comes a point in life where you must move on, step up to the plate, and get it done. My background has helped me deal with kids in all sorts of bad situations over the years. The mix of pushing and sympathy is key to mentoring because it's what kids need.

My message to my players has always been "it's okay to be the good guy" and that means in all areas of athletics and life. It is okay to be a good student, it is okay to be a good teammate, it is okay to be a good person, it is okay to love your parents and show affection, it is okay to be well mannered, it is okay to say no, it is okay to respect people, it is okay to make decisions that are right, and the list goes on and on. They need to know they're strong enough to achieve their goals because they've got someone in their corner.

HUDDLE UP WITH TOM THOMPSON:
WHEN LIFE IS YOUR MENTOR

When we think about mentors, we traditionally think about someone more experienced, perhaps a little older than we are, who shares their time, talent, and expertise to help us navigate life's up and downs. But coaches and mentors aren't always *people*. Sometimes life itself can be our biggest mentor and our strongest coach.

The situations that life throws against us are the crucible for refining our character. I'd never considered that my life would go any way other than how I'd planned it out late in high school. I didn't know the fine points, but I knew what the broad strokes would be, which basically consisted of football and partying. Yet, as much as I believed I was destined for college football, God had a different plan for me.

Choosing Family over Football

In February of my senior year, in 1968, I found out that my father was sick and undergoing cancer treatments in Dallas. Technically, Dad's residence was in Mexico at that time because he was trying to get a Mexican divorce, but he was traveling back and forth for cancer treatments. I couldn't bear going off to play college football somewhere when my mind was constantly on my dad. I offered to come to Dallas to take care of him, but my father wasn't too keen on that idea at all. I don't think he wanted me to see him sick. So to honor his wishes, I stayed in Florida and tried to cope with not being able to see him regularly or know what was going on with his treatments.

In August or September, about the time kids head off to college, Dad took a turn for the worse, and by November he was back in the hospital in Dallas, where he would stay until the end. I tried to follow his wishes and go to college. I wanted to attend Lenoir-Rhyne College (now University) in Hickory, North Carolina, but that seemed too far away, so I enrolled in classes at St. Petersburg Junior College. What started out at nine hours of coursework was quickly whittled down to three. I didn't care about academics. Class work was an end to play football and that wasn't possible. Plus, I was worried about my dad, and nothing else really seemed to matter that much.

My father passed away in January of 1969. I was still living with my aunt and uncle, and was still enrolled in SPJC, but had stopped attending classes. I got through that first semester before I dropped out. I thought my best course of action would have been to work for a bit and try to gain some direction, or at least some financial security. I had inherited some money from my father, but it wouldn't be given to me until I was twenty-one and I was only nineteen when he died. So I decided I could try college again once I got my inheritance and had some breathing space financially.

Fumbling through Life

In anticipation of returning to college in 1970, I first talked to Southern Methodist. My grand plan was that I would attempt to walk on at SMU. But since I had been out of football for a couple of years, SMU arranged for me to play at Northwood University outside of Dallas. Pending a successful season, I was to then transfer to SMU on a scholarship. So I met with Northwood's coach in the spring semester, and he agreed to let me walk on the team the next fall. I immediately started training and continued through summer. My dream of playing college football was going to happen, and I had to be ready for it! Then, in the fall, the unthinkable happened. Northwood University dropped their football program. *How could this happen? I* had done all of the things I was supposed to do, and the way before me was blocked.

At the same time, I was newly married and had started working in the import business. Even though this door had been slammed shut, football was still always in the back of my mind, but for the moment, I had a life to live. Football didn't ring true to me anymore, or so I convinced myself of that.

The next time I thought about playing football was in the United States Football League (USFL). If you blinked in the early 1980s, you might have missed the USFL. It was conceived as a summer football league and ran for three seasons before folding. I was going to try to make a USFL team as a punter, and I worked out with that goal in mind for a while. Once again, life got in the way. I thought the closest I would ever get to being involved with football was when I was working for the Dallas Cowboys for five years. There was no real traction to any of my own attempts to return to football, but I always loved the game and deep down, I still wanted to play.

When I was younger, even after my dad left, there wasn't a coach who ruffled my hair and patted me on the back. "You can do it, Tom. I believe in you," would have been wonderful words to hear, but such words were rarely ever spoken to me when I was failing my way through college, or in the early 1980s when the USFL crossed my mind.

Maybe things would have been different if I'd had a few mentors to guide me through some of my challenges and decisions. But through my near misses with football, there was only one man who actively mentored me, and he was only a few years older than I was. Larry Rudisill Sr. coached me during my junior and senior years of high school. He'd often say of me, "Thompson plays like a poor boy." I knew what that meant; poor boys play hard. He championed me at every turn, reaching out to colleges to try to get scholarships for me. And he was successful. I'd have several opportunities to play college football—until my decision to stay close during my dad's illness changed the trajectory of my path. I would eventually get back out on the field, though much later than I'd anticipated.

My most prominent and consistent coach and mentor for my football journey (and my life's journey) was life itself. Every time a door was shut on my football dreams, another one would open. The length between opportunities might have been years, if not decades, but football was still being put on my radar. To this day, I believe those opportunities were from God. The lesson I finally learned from this is that God is testing our hearts (Psalm 37:4).

God Is the Ultimate Coach

Coach Wilson was surely moved by his God-given gifts to influence Ronnie Gage. The culmination of Wilson's life experiences and open heart allowed him to touch the life of Ronnie Gage and other young people in positive and affirming ways. Ronnie's decision to become a coach was based on the love and caring he received from those dedicated men. By the efforts of Coach Wilson and Coach Bogue, and Ronnie's other mentors, they touched countless lives though Coach Gage's work. Because of the example set for him, Ronnie Gage knew how to open his heart and eyes to the kids that were put in his path.

We often turn to God only when there are no other mentors or teachers available and no answers available to the questions burning in our hearts. He puts teachable situations in our path every day that answer our prayers and needs. We must only open our eyes to those moments to let the Lord be our mentor. He always listens to you, but do you listen to Him? I bet he's drawing up a game-changing play for you right now.

3

Grade-School Crush

Mentoring and coaching don't always happen on the ball field and aren't always about one's performance as an athlete. The bedrock of my life's work has been my wife, Stephanie. She's literally always been there. We started school at the same time, and she caught my eye in the second grade. We cut up and played together during elementary school recesses. In junior high, Stephane and I became sweethearts. That status didn't last into high school, though, when Stephanie left me for an upperclassman and started dating someone else.

Meeting Stephanie

I hadn't gotten anywhere on the playing field without persistence, so I used the same tactic with Stephanie. I repeatedly asked her out, and she kept turning me down. Has someone ever caught your eye and you just know? I knew Stephanie was the one a long time ago, so I asked her out one more time. But even with my tenacious streak, there comes a point when you've done all you can. I declared to a buddy, "I'm done—I'm not going to ask her out anymore." Saying that to someone made it reality I had to stick to. Then, one day I opened my locker and inside was a note that read: "I apologize for the way I've been acting. I really do think I'd like to go out with you if you'd give me another chance." I still have that note.

I thought about the dimples that formed when Stephanie flashed her smile. I thought about just how intelligent she was. I thought about how I *just knew.* I gave Stephanie another chance, and we've been together ever since. We went to our junior and senior proms together. She even became the bookkeeper of the basketball team just so

1971, Ronnie and Stephanie were high school sweethearts.

we could spend more time together. That's the perfect example of how Stephanie has helped me find a way to achieve my professional goals while growing our relationship.

Is it any wonder our fortieth wedding anniversary happened while I was preparing this book? I have no idea where the time has gone, and I wouldn't have it any other way.

Encouraging Each Other and Making It Work

Finding "the one" doesn't mean there won't be hard times. Stephanie and I had our share of trials and tribulations after we graduated from high school in 1971. She went to Austin and I headed for Texas Tech. We were nine hours away from each other that year. Long-distance relationships at that age are tough. It was even tougher then, when communications were through the mail or after pumping dimes into a pay phone.

My first year at Tech didn't work out the way I wanted it to. It was hard to focus, so I came home, worked, and went to Weatherford Junior College. Leaving Tech and coming home was the smartest move I ever made in my education. Being in familiar surroundings helped me get my act together to focus on school and my future.

Stephanie, on the other hand, was always organized, focused, and good at planning. As we long-distance dated through college, we'd talk about what came next for us. Once I moved back home, it allowed us to spend more time together.

We went on a picnic our senior year of high school and mapped out our futures as best we could. She had always wanted to become a nurse. There weren't many career choices for women in the 1960s and early '70s, and nursing was a solid choice for Stephanie. I held firm to becoming a coach, and that day we looked at how to make it work.

Deciding to Become a Coach

In my final years of high school, I knew I wasn't good enough in any one sport to compete on the next level. That odd combination of a pole-vaulting, basketball dribbling, 150-pound center, and safety wasn't the makeup college recruiters were looking for. However, sports did get me though high school. I didn't enjoy most academic subjects and hated going to class. Yet my love of sports motivated me to graduate from college so that I could coach one day. I even finished my education with a master's degree, because it helped me to advance my coaching career ladder.

If the impact sports had on my life was to keep me in school and propel my life forward, I wanted to enable that to happen for others. I saw what coaches had done for me and my friends, and I knew it was my job to give back by doing something I truly enjoyed.

All young people need discipline and leadership, but unless you have a strict household, there's not a lot of places that teach mental and physical discipline, outside of the military—except for athletics. Participating in team sports is the one accessible place where kids can be taught lessons that will help them the rest of their lives.

In addition to keeping in touch with a few of my former coaches, I'm still in contact with several of my high school classmates. They all say the same thing. We grew up having a great time while receiving the guidance we needed to become good adults, all because of our parents and our coaches.

I wanted to be *that coach*. It's a calling and as honorable profession as any that have ever existed. Everything about coaching appealed to me. I could stay involved with the competition that I loved so much while helping others. It was a win-win in my mind.

Back in the late 1960s, there was no way to see just how important good coaches would become in our society. Kids need coaching now more than ever. Family dynamics and home economics have changed so dramatically coaches often give guidance where parents or guardians can't or won't.

It takes two incomes to make most households work these days, and this may make it difficult for parents and guardians to attend their kid's practices or even games. That's where coaches must step in with a little more encouragement and pride in an athlete's achievements. Those things go a long way for kids and lay the foundation that makes for successful adults.

Landing My Dream Job

Entering the adult world was exactly what Stephanie and I had talked about during that senior year picnic. I graduated college in 1976 with a health and physical education degree, and Stephanie had become a nurse a year earlier, in 1975. We never attended the same college, and time and distance have a way of wearing a relationship down. I knew that if I didn't ask Stephanie to marry me, I might lose her.

We got married in August 1977, and she worked at Children's Medical Center for four years. Then she taught nursing at Texas Woman's University (TWU) for four more years. During that time, Jessica and Juli were born, and Stephanie had a great idea on how to make our life work with a growing family.

Now, I mentioned how my wife is intelligent, and she jumped on the idea of school nursing. She could become the nurse at whichever school I was coaching at. That way we could both support each other's careers and we'd have summers together. Her plan worked better than I could have imagined.

My first job was in the Keller school district as a junior high coach, and we lived in Grapevine, Texas. I wanted to move up the ladder and to reach my goal of becoming a varsity coach, but the district couldn't find anything to further my ambitions. In 1978, I got a call from my old coach, Neal Wilson. He wanted me to be his assistant coach at Lewisville. That was a dream come true for me.

It's funny how we sometimes don't appreciate things or people until they're about to leave us. Right after the folks in Keller caught wind of the move, my boss asked, "Hey, I think we are going to be able to work this out. Why don't you call Coach Wilson and tell him you are going to stay here and coach?"

I said, "No, I wouldn't do that. He means too much to me, and I have given him my word and I am going to go."

You never know how things are going to turn out. But twenty-three years at Lewisville ISD, two state championships, fifteen years as a head coach, and one year as full-time athletic director—I think I made a good decision by accepting Coach Wilson's offer. Just to be able to carry my career under Neal Wilson's tutelage was a crowning achievement. God put me in this position and gave me the strength and wisdom to succeed.

In 1991, I'd go on to become the head coach at Lewisville High School, and Neal was now the athletic director. No matter what Neal Wilson's title, he'd always be a coach to me. Coach Wilson was a wise, sentimental, understanding man, who was very well thought of in the community. I wasn't afraid to go in and sit down to ask for his advice on any life topic. He always found the time for me, even though he was in charge of five high schools and fourteen junior highs.

Coach Wilson died of leukemia over ten years ago. I miss seeing him and having our conversations. I learned a lot from him over the years, and I also learned some things I would do differently. That's what coaching, mentoring, and family is about. Creating relationships strong and honest enough to weather good and bad times.

While I am not saying Coach Wilson took on the role of being my dad, having him around over the years took the sting out of

Being a father is the most important role I will ever play and if I don't do this well, no other thing I do really matters.

2011, Ronnie's philosophy on being a good father.

not having my dad around. He gave me my first opportunity to really grow as a coach, and in a way, we became part of each other's family. To this day, his wife and middle son, Lance, are close. I coached Lance as a young man and am still close to his family. In fact, Mrs. Wilson and Lance came to my last game at Paradise High School, and that meant the world to me. Even though Coach Wilson couldn't be there, his presence was felt through his wife and son. Family endures like that.

Becoming a Father

When we married, Stephanie and I knew that we wanted children, so we were thrilled when Jessica was born in 1981. Juli was born in 1985, and our family of four was perfect! We hadn't decided if we wanted a third child but God knew that we needed James in our lives so we were blessed with him in 1987. They are the greatest gifts God could ever have given Stephanie and me.

Jess was a tiny thing when she was born and boy, could she cry! There were many nights Jess and I rocked in the rocker. When she wanted to be held, she would say, "Rock that baby," repeating what her parents often said. I would gladly get her, and we would go and rock in the chair until she fell asleep. She was always an expressive child and a breath of fresh air. Her beautiful smile could light up a room, and she had a gift of making people feel good about themselves. She loved her family and she loved life. Her fight and fortitude gave us the motivation to move forward.

Juli, being born the middle child, learned to fend for herself at an early age. She has always been independent and strong and knows just what she wants and when. She, too, has a smile that can warm your heart. She is a champion of the underdog and is not afraid to stand up for anything that she thinks is right. She is a "no fear" person and a fierce competitor. She's a leader and gets a lot out of people. She chose to become a coach too, of volleyball, cross country, and track, and she is girl's coordinator at her high school. I've told several people she may be the best coach in the family.

As the baby, James's sisters knew how to get him to do anything and were always pushing his buttons. He adored his sisters! He was laid back since birth and driven by sports at a young age. He would play with anything that involved a ball. Like me, James always knew that he wanted to coach. James is a phenomenal person because he is such a people person. He can go in a room with fifty people and in an hour come out knowing forty-nine of them. He has a lot to offer as a coach because he is a good person and a great competitor.

We were very fortunate with all our children. They are beautiful kids, and Stephanie and I have been the proudest people in the world.

We've also discovered that parenting isn't much different than coaching. You have to wake up every morning with your game face on because your kids need you. That's not something you can take a day off from or tell them you'll get to them when you have time. They have an expectation for you to lead them as a parent and you set your expectations on their development as people. That's the best 24/7 job ever created, tantrums, diapers, and all.

HUDDLE UP WITH TOM THOMPSON:
FINDING A TEAMMATE IN A SOUL MATE

From the age of twenty-four until I was about forty, I tried to live a good life. I held fast to being a good guy. I did everything that I thought I was supposed to do, but nothing ever ended or changed. There was never a linear progression to my life. I knew something was missing, but I didn't know what it was. I remember one day crying out to God and saying, "I need reality to my faith. I need there to be something tangible to this."

I also knew I was not living a victorious life. The proof was that I was going through my fourth divorce. *Was I so off-base that I couldn't put my act together?* At that time in my life, I didn't understand how it all worked. I was doing everything I knew to do, exhausting all my ideas and resources, but nothing was changing. It would take more time and a few ordained experiences before I realized I'm not the one who puts my life together anyway, He is. As is often happens, God was about to throw me a curveball that I didn't know I needed.

The Calling of the Cross

In all the church teachings that I had been around, which weren't very many, I heard that charismatic people were crazy, demon-possessed people. I soon learned that one of my friends attended a local charismatic church; he was the president of a bank located in a building I managed. We had become friends through the real estate, but he took a true interest in me. As our friendship grew, he told me he was praying for me and a little more about charismatic Christianity. I was skeptical, of course. He seemed so . . . normal.

Right around the time of my fourth divorce, another friend suggested that if I wanted to learn more about what God was about, I really needed to attend a charismatic church, and at least give it a try. There was that word again: *charismatic*. My mind filled with over-exaggerated ideas of what I thought that would look like. I did not want to go, but as hesitant as I was to step through those doors, I knew I was at a crossroads in my life. Even with my limited knowledge of faith, I remember thinking, "Success is one thing, but it is nothing if it is not blessed of God." I wanted His blessing, but I didn't know how to receive it. I hope it didn't have to come through shouting, speaking in tongues, and grabbing snakes. In fact, if I saw one snake at all, I was going to levitate from my seat faster than a hot knife through butter.

The first time I set foot in a charismatic church, during one portion of the service there was a communal prayer that ended with speaking in tongues. What started out as a murmuring stream of voices swelled into a river of noise I couldn't comprehend. At that point, I realized I had to leave early. And fast. There was this thing I had to do and I just remembered. No snakes required!

I don't know why, but I went back. Maybe it was because I was curious or maybe there was an internal pull I didn't recognize, but I started out on the very back row. That way, if things got *really nuts*, I wanted out in a hurry. Then I slowly but surely made my way to about the middle of the church, and it was like the Holy Spirit said, "If you want to see if I'm real, stick around." And, well, I've always liked a challenge.

Signs from Above

It took me a couple of weeks before I fell under conviction in the service. When I did, I wept freely and walked to the front of the church. The pastor met me and put his hands on either side of my neck. "Sir, get your life in order," was all he said.

Unbeknownst to me, standing behind the pastor was a woman named Teresa. She was singing, and once I finally saw her, I realized both her voice and her beauty were captivating. In fact, I would eventually marry her. I think back on that day from time to time and realize how symbolic it all was. There, standing in front of me, was a man of God and behind the man of God was my future wife. Teresa had her own life challenges before meeting me, but we were able to come together to overcome it all. We balance each other. She's my best friend. My soulmate. My helper, encourager, and the glue that holds our family together.

Optimism is a choice, just as love is a choice. I am an optimist overall, based on my faith. I also see places in the Bible that say things are going to get worse in this world, not better. Ultimately, the only optimism I have is with Jesus. It isn't with what is going on in the world. However, Teresa has a way of always seeing the good in people. In her eyes, people are kindhearted and good until they prove to be otherwise.

A Partnership Built on God's Foundation

Just like Ronnie and Stephanie are a team, Teresa and I are a team. We value each other's opinions and respect the other as an equal. If Teresa is not in complete agreement with me on any decision, I won't do it. I don't care how glittery the end result of that decision is. And she respects my opinions and decisions as well. Our respect goes both ways. A good marriage is not about asking permission; it's about sustaining a partnership.

I had prayed for someone in my life like Teresa, and when I least expected it, she was there in front of me. He is still answering my prayers today.

As I have gotten older, the more I believe God's Word and the less of the world I hang onto. It often causes me to have a different perspective than I did in my twenties and thirties. Because I'm getting older, some of the things I still want to achieve need to hurry up and happen, at least in my mind. But the "hurrying up" part is me hanging on to a timeline of my choosing. God often has a different plan and says, "No, you need to follow my lead. Be patient and do not worry about when."

Teresa helps me keep to God's timeline instead of my own, and why wouldn't she? The way she came into my life made it obvious she would be my helpmate in spiritual matters. Ronnie and Stephanie have that same type of relationship. Walking together in the day-to-day decisions of life makes a marriage easier. Walking together in the Lord, that gets couples through the worst of times, and allows them to more fully celebrate and appreciate the good times.

4

Coaching Your Own Kids

As a coach, the biggest thing you worry about if you're also a parent is spending enough quality time with your own family. This is especially true when your kids are young. It's easy to miss any of the important firsts when juggling any career, but I encourage you to attend as many school and athletic events as you can and make your family a priority. Your kids will never understand all the sacrifices you made to be there for them, but they'll always remember seeing your face in the audience and feeling loved.

Coaching is a demanding career for many reasons. Aside from the details and logistics of running a team, there are always parents with difficult personalities and ever-changing school district

2001, Julianne, James, and Jessica.

requirements. I had the added pressure of being at a large high school with a successful program. If you're going to be good at coaching or anything else, you've got to work at it. There are no shortcuts or shortchanges. But that also comes with higher expectations. Everyone wants a piece of your time and everyone wants to share their opinion of how they think you should be doing your job.

Being a Coach 24/7

Stephanie and I both knew we would have to exert the same principles of teamwork I taught on the field to not shortchange our own children at home. My wife was a tremendous help in getting kids here and there when I couldn't. Stephanie would come to my games with one child on her arm and the other two at her side. She was as talented at wrangling our children as any cowboy I'd ever seen.

We would always manage to get involved with Little League, recitals, concerts, and the other activities they were in, all through their younger days. Whatever was going on, one of us or both of us were there. That was a commitment we made to each other and to our children because I knew I couldn't be a coach to my children if I wasn't there.

As much as we were involved in our children's lives, they were also involved in my professional life. Being the child of a coach, or the spouse of a coach, is as much of a job as being a parent. Still, every game I coached, Stephanie and the kids were there.

When the kids were in youth sports, most of their games were in the summer or weekends. I tried to be at as many of their games as work allowed, and even helped coach when possible. Stephanie was always there, too. Sometimes we had two kids in two games at different places and one parent went each way. When Juli was on the varsity volleyball team in high school, her games were on Friday nights at the same time as my games, so Stephanie went to Juli's games, and as soon as they were over, they drove to my football games, sometimes getting there late in the fourth quarter, but they were determined to come anyway.

1992, Family was always on field after a game, win or lose.

Train Them Up When They're Young

When James was six, he wanted to get on my sideline during games. He was too young to be there, and I always worried about him getting hurt. An out-of-bounds play or incomplete pass would have seriously injured the little man. But one cold, bitter night, I let him come on the sidelines to stand near me. Rivulets of sleet were blowing here and there, stinging our exposed faces. But James didn't care. He was having the time of his little chilly life!

We were winning at halftime, and my wife met me down by the field house to ask if James could come in the locker room to warm up. I agreed, and when it was time to go back for the second half,

James asked if he could stay on the sidelines. I assigned a trainer to watch him right before we kicked off. He was allowed to be the "tee boy" which meant he got to retrieve the tee from the field after the kickoff.

James was beaming with pride when he told his mother after the game, "Dad let me come down there and that was great. I got to go out on the field and get that kicking tee. On the way out there, I think I had a tear in my eye I was so excited." Stephanie told me what he said and from then on, James was on the sidelines with me. So, he grew up on the sidelines, in the fieldhouse, and around the guys and the coaches. (It's no wonder he became a coach himself.)

Jess and Juli experienced a portion of my coaching life while they were growing up, too. Jess was a cheerleader and down in the center of it all. Juli was her mom's sidekick in the stands when she was younger, and they would sit together during the game on Friday nights to cheer our team on. When she was older, she sat with the "Rowdy Crowd" if she wasn't playing volleyball. She loved to be the first one on the field to greet me after a football game, win or lose.

Stephanie and I enjoyed some unexpected benefits from our children due to our close involvement with their sports and school. Our house was always open and full of kids and players. Jess, Juli, and James each had a group of friends that were wonderfully close to them, and Stephanie and I considered them ours too. To this day, their friends are like our extended family. I think Stephanie and I had as much fun with their friends as they did growing up. What a blessing to constantly have a house of merriment and a safe place for so many kids to enjoy.

School was a good experience for all of them, but it was harder with both parents working at the same school they attended. They couldn't get away with anything! Stephanie and I sometimes worried that because we were faculty, our children would feel like they were being scrutinized. Everybody in the school knew everything about our kids, and the teachers were looking out for them. Plus, they knew we wanted them to live up to expectations that we had for the classroom and on the practice field. Were their friends reporting back what was going on with boyfriends or girlfriends just to get on the coach's good side?

I do think we guarded against that enough that it didn't affect the kids. I'm sure there are pros and cons to being around your family 24/7, but in the end, I think they enjoyed the title of being a coach's kid. In a letter they wrote me when I was still coaching in Lewisville, they said "We will always be your biggest fans and we will always be coaches' kids. Thanks for giving that to us. We couldn't be more proud of you."

The Good and Bad of Coaching Your Own Kids

I knew the biggest challenge of all would come if I had to coach my own children. The girls, of course, would not fall in my football program, although I did find out that I was a great sideline volleyball coach when Juli started playing. I didn't know the first thing about volleyball, but suddenly I turned into an expert. I didn't think anything about it, but I was coaching the hound out of it just like the other parents do. I loved watching her compete in volleyball and track in the spring. I was so proud of her strong work ethic and competitiveness.

I didn't have that problem with Jess. Bless her heart, we tried to make an athlete out of her, but she wasn't as athletically gifted as her siblings. She ran track in her freshman year, and after one particularly unsuccessful race, I went down to talk to her. Before I could say a word, she said, "Dad, don't even go there. I know I suck and I'm not going to do this anymore. So, don't tell me I did a good job." I laughed because she was just as adamant as she could be.

She did get involved in cheerleading and did that for four years. Two of those years she attended the National Cheerleading Competition. Jess was talented in her own way, even if it wasn't in the way I had initially envisioned. I was impressed and extremely proud of her!

I was particularly worried about the prospects of coaching James. He was so passionate about football and a good enough athlete I was pretty sure he would make the team. I think it was harder for James to play for me than it was for me to coach him. There was always a target on James's back.

At times it didn't matter how good or bad he was. If he played too much, I was showing favoritism. If he struggled, the peanut gallery would say he shouldn't have made the team in the first place. I was going to be second-guessed no matter how I coached my son. There were times I wanted to grab him by the shoulders, and I had trouble deciding whether to get after him or to hug him. It was usually a toss-up as to which. But with all things, I navigated it as best I could. James always managed to find his way on the football field and the baseball diamond and contributed well as a Fighting Farmer in both sports. He went on to play four years of baseball at Hardin Simmons University in Abilene, where he had a great deal of success.

2004, On field, celebration of Ronnie's retirement from Lewisville High School in 2004. With Julianne and Jessica.

Stephanie and I formed as close a bond with our children as we could during their formative years by simply being present. We took every opportunity we could for us to be together as a family. My biggest challenge was not making all of the dentist appointments or being there to kiss all the skinned knees. We had to navigate the many years of teenage angst and teaching the kids how to drive.

I had to remember that being a father is like being a coach, but I didn't always have to be a coach to be a father. I had, and have to now, watch myself about being overbearing and demanding. Even with guarding against that, I still catch myself preaching to Juli and James about trivial matters, and both my children are over thirty and successful by their own rights. Here I am, still the dad and head coach, telling them how to do things. They've both gotten pretty good about putting me in my place if I step out of bounds. I'm glad I've taught them to have a backbone and to stand up when it's necessary.

They Call Me "Coach"

For Father's Day one year, my grown kids gave me a book they put together. Inside were letters from kids, parents, and coaches that I have worked with over the years. I couldn't believe my children had gone to the trouble of organizing it. I also was humbled that all those people took the time to write.

In all those letters, I kept seeing the word, "coach" used as if it were my name. It might have well been my name. That's what I am from the time I get up in the morning until bedtime. I am proud of that title. I belong to an honorable profession that my son and daughter are part of too.

I hope to be able to teach all the same values and lessons I taught my children to my grandchildren. Everyone always asked me,

"When your grandkids are born, what are they going to call you?"

I said, "They are going to call me 'Coach.'"

My grandkids actually call me, "Coach" and Stephanie "Pokey." I'll take it. That means that I can be their coach, just like I was their parents' coach. The time I'll spend with my grandchildren will be different than it was when I coached James, Jess, and Juli. Instead, Stephanie and I will take our grandchildren to their parents' games. With James as a head football coach and athletic director and Juli as a head track coach and girl's coordinator, I'll be able to sit in the stands and explain what's going on to my grandchildren. This is a coaching family, and I'll take however much time I need to support my kids and grandkids in all they do.

HUDDLE UP WITH TOM THOMPSON:
DEEP IN THE HEART OF TEXAS

If you're not from Texas, you should know that around here, football is treated like no other sport or activity. There is a reverence for football that doesn't exist for hunting, soccer, or baseball. Football is taught, talked about, and dissected on a level that would make nuclear engineers wonder at the methodology. If you don't understand football, you simply don't understand Texas.

Other states will claim to have the level of enthusiasm for football that we do, but they'd be wrong. States like Florida, California, Pennsylvania, and Ohio are known to produce good football players, but nothing like Texas. I'm convinced there are pigskin genes in a Texan's DNA.

The passion for football takes hold early and remains a lifelong commitment. In most other states, you'd attend a high school football game if your own child was playing. On Friday nights, the stands of Texas high school games are packed with members of the community because football is a stitch in the fabric of any town.

Texans follow high school football games like other states follow college games. For example, upwards of 200,000 people will follow the Texas high school football state championship. That is a lot of people, and one of the reasons that championship used to be held in the Astrodome, which maxed out at 67,925 seats. That number represents nearly four times the attendance and viewership of any other state's championship games. They say everything is bigger in Texas, but numbers like that are all that's needed to tell the story.

For the Texans reading this text, you know exactly what I'm talking about. This explanation is more for those not graced by the good Lord to have experienced the reality of Texas football. One must understand the commitment Texans hold to the game to understand Ronnie Gage, and what it means to be a football coach in Texas.

The Pressure Starts Young

The state is the first stop for college recruiters from across the country. Generally, a Texas football player is going to stay in the region. Sometimes players will jump ship and go to Stanford or other elite schools, but that has been the exception.

Recruiting happens all the time within the NCAA rules, and National Signing Day marks the end of the recruiting trail. Those players can be signed by colleges starting their junior year. Colleges can offer scholarships at any time, but they can't be accepted until the junior year. For example, someone as young as twelve years old could be offered a scholarship from a recruiter at Michigan. But it doesn't make sense to sign a kid until you know how good a player they are going to mature into. The younger kids who are offered scholarships are outliers. Still, that's what the recruiters are looking for, the phenoms.

College is becoming more expensive for a working-class family.

A football scholarship might be the only way a family could send their son to school. That's the reason pee-wee leagues have become so popular. If a child waits to start playing football in junior high school, they've already lost their shot at standing out among teammates who have already been playing for ten years. There are fifty other kids that have been running drills since they were nine. Then there are parents who try to breathe down a coach's neck for playing time or who demand special treatment for their children.

This is the coaching landscape Coach Gage has navigated for years. That's why statements like "making sure the kids have fun" might sound outdated by today's standards. But that's exactly why it's such a necessary message. Kids should be allowed to be kids and develop their skills and interests without unnecessary pressure. And that's the same coaching approach I've used with my own son, Jon Rawles, as well as the college kickers.

I'm happy to pull a player along, encouraging and coaching to their potential, but I won't push anyone into a sport. Since I'm not trying to live my life through my son's athletic ability, I'm letting Jon Rawles dictate which sports he does, because I want him to have fun. Whatever footsteps he wants to take, that's what I'm going to help him do.

Since Austin College doesn't give out athletic-based scholarships, I have to assume that all my players are there because they *genuinely want to be there*. With the kickers, I make sure they are confident in their fundamentals. At that point, I let them find themselves and I coach and correct when I see an opportunity to add value to what they're currently doing. I believe this not only fosters confidence in the kickers, but also self-leadership and camaraderie among the players. Because in good times and in bad, you need to be able to rely on your team, to celebrate the wins and to shoulder the disappointments together.

5

The Pain No Parent
Should Know

I have learned over the years that pain can be easier to talk about than to ignore, even when that's all you want to do. I've also learned that you can make all the time you can for your family, but that's not always enough. In some situations, time runs out before you want it to. That's why I talk about what happened to Jess. To remind me, and those who will listen, that *you've got to make time,* because you're not promised tomorrow.

Jess went off to college like a lot of teenagers, not knowing what she wanted to be when she graduated. She didn't have the calling for coaching like I had, and nothing felt right, she couldn't find something she wanted to turn into a career. She ended up taking a semester off, and Stephanie and I didn't find out about it until Jess had already withdrawn from classes. That just absolutely killed Stephanie, who would have made a career out of school if she could have. Stephanie reads all the time and loved the challenge of a classroom environment. Jess was like me and didn't enjoy the classroom at all.

Stephanie was too devastated to talk to Jess objectively about her education, so I took over shepherding her through the process.

I wasn't happy with Jess's choices but as a good father would do, I helped her get her act together.

When Jess Got Sick

Jess had just enrolled in classes again when everything went sideways. At the time, she was living in a Dallas suburb. She had been plagued by migraines around that time, but she was under stress with the return to school, and assumed they'd pass once things settled down. Except in Jess's case, they got worse.

In late November 2006, we received a call that she had been taken to the emergency room with seizures. A CAT scan revealed that there was some bleeding in Jess's brain. The bleeding wasn't indicative of a stroke, but the kind of bleeding associated with tumors. There was a neurosurgeon on call in the hospital, and after examining her scan, he told us that Jess had a brain tumor that was possibly malignant and would need to be surgically removed immediately. You can imagine the impact of those words on us as parents. We were sure that he had jumped to conclusions and probably misdiagnosed her medical condition, so we sought a second opinion from another neurosurgeon the hospital nurses had suggested.

We set up an appointment with him and based on the CAT scan, his initial diagnosis was a cavernous hemangioma malformation, which is a blood vessel malformation. This was a benign lesion. The doctor described the small mass like a grapevine that had little vessels at the end. Every now and then, one of the vessels would bleed. His advice was that if it bleeds again, he would go in and remove it. If there was no bleeding, the vessel had closed itself off. But in his opinion, Jess wouldn't have any problems in either case. The surgical option sounded as simple as taking out her tonsils or appendix, so we waited. You can imagine the relief that we felt. This

*1995, Ronnie, Stephanie, and Jessica on sideline after game.
Holding up the "L."*

was a much better diagnosis than the first, and we thought that life would be able to move on normally.

Sure enough, in February 2007, Jess experienced a cranial hemorrhage again so the neurosurgeon from the second consult said it was time for surgery. Surgery was scheduled, and at this time, we all still thought he would be repairing the cavernous hemangioma.

Gut Check

I had an uneasy feeling the morning of the surgery. My stomach flopped and the butterflies wouldn't quit. I just didn't feel good about things, but there was no explaining it. I was nervous for Jess, but this . . . this was something different.

Jess was in surgery for several hours before the doctor came back out to speak with us. He didn't even have to say anything—we knew bad news was coming by his expression. *Glioblastoma* was a word I'd probably never heard before that day and wished I never had. It wasn't a benign lesion like we had hoped and prayed. My little girl had the granddaddy of all brain tumors, a glioblastoma multiforme, or GBM. This is a very aggressive, fast-growing tumor with a poor prognosis. The doctor tried to explain the implications of GBM, but he was shaken and used lots of medical terminology that was hard to absorb, because we had just been given devastating news. We had a waiting room full of family and friends who had come to support us, and you can imagine how the air was sucked out of the room with this diagnosis. It didn't take long for all of us to understand just had bad GBM was.

It wasn't just our family that was devastated; Jess had a serious boyfriend named Bo, who was with her when the initial seizure occurred. He and his family were in the waiting room too and, of course, the news was a huge blow for him. Bo stayed with Jess throughout the entire illness, two-and-a-half years, and they got married in December 2007. About a hundred people attended her wedding, and there wasn't a dry eye in the chapel as the beautiful bride walked down the aisle to join her beloved Bo in marriage. He

1997, Ronnie and his girls who were always first to find him after a game.

became Jess's rock and best cheerleader and never gave up hope for her recovery. He just knew she would be the one to beat the odds.

After the surgery in February, Jess found a wonderful neuro-oncologist at Southwestern Medical Center to follow her care. The plan was to hold off on chemotherapy and radiation until monthly MRIs showed if the tumor returned. It did. In October 2007, Jessica had her second surgery and then started twenty-eight days of radiation and chemotherapy.

There was hope in the beginning, but that dwindled during Jess's two-and-a-half-year battle. She fought as hard as anyone could. Even in the hospital after both surgeries, Jess had a way of making people feel good about themselves. The doctors and nurses loved her and fought the disease alongside her.

The Family Pulled Together

There were many people in Jess's corner who helped—including her sister Juli. She had graduated from Texas A&M in 2007 with the eventual intention of teaching and coaching. I say eventual because she thought becoming a flight attendant for a couple of years after college would be a great way to see the world. But airlines aren't quite setup as a working travel agency, and she was stationed in Newark, New Jersey, when Jess started getting worse. She quit in January 2009 and came home and moved in with Jess and Bo so that she could help.

For five months, Juli stayed by Jess's side, even though she had taken a new job at TXU Energy. She had bosses who knew the situation with her sister, so they allowed her to take time off whenever she was needed. Juli was a silent hero in Jess's story. She worked tirelessly with Bo to make Jess as comfortable as possible during her last months and basically put her life on hold to be there for her sister. James was finishing his senior year in college, and at the end of the semester he came home to help too. It was a family affair. At times, there were six of us living in Jess and Bo's house with the intent of being there every minute that we could and helping make Jess's life the easiest it could be.

In January 2009, when Jess's health started to decline, Stephanie and I were still trying to work. Stephanie had moved in with Jess and Bo, and her work was about thirty minutes from their house. She continued to work for a couple of months and then took a leave of absence for the last few months. I was working at Austin College and drove to Jess and Bo's house every day after work—about a seventy-five-minute drive one way. Then every night I drove back to Sherman so that I could work the next day, which was again, a seventy-five-minute return trip. I never missed a day. We were so fortunate to have employers who supported us and allowed us to concentrate on our daughter while they covered things at work. Neither of us wanted to leave her side.

It was tragic in the end. Jess had lost use of her right leg and right arm. She lost her voice and couldn't speak, so we had to learn a new way to communicate with her. It was so hard to watch. As a dad, you are supposed to be able to protect your family. I searched and tried everything I knew to find an answer. There just wasn't one there.

Then on June 4, 2009, at 1:00 a.m., Jess went to her eternal home.

After weeks of intense grief, Stephanie told me one day, "We still have two beautiful kids. We can't let this take them away from us. We have to move on and live for them." We had to remember that her siblings lost their sister, and their grief was as great as ours.

My wife was right. Eventually, you surrender your anger and put your faith in God. He will walk you through it. You have to learn to accept that God had a plan for Jess. It just wasn't the same plan that we desired. We had to dig deep in our life-long faith to find our way back to trusting God. You work things out with the Lord's help. In that way, we have come to terms with Jess's death.

The loss of my daughter is something I have accepted, but at times it is just as devastating as the day she left. Even today, there are times when out of nowhere, the grief will jump up and grab me around the throat and suffocate me. A song, a scent, something will trigger that emotional avalanche. It is not something that anybody should ever have to go through, but we walk through it day by day, sometimes hour by hour.

One way of dealing with my grief was to be there for my family and to be as supportive as I knew how. Jess's husband Bo was hit every bit as hard as Stephanie and I were. I told Bo one day after it was all over with, "You're young. At some point, you are going to have to move on with your life. Don't ever let the Gages stand in your way." Jess's husband had done everything he was supposed to do, and now it was time to let him go too.

Bo has remarried and has a little girl. He and his parents join us in the Brain Tumor Walk every year in the fall. We still have a great relationship with them, and that's a blessing. Jess started us on this Walk in 2008 and was able to participate as a survivor for one year. We have vowed to continue, annually, in her memory and help raise money for brain tumor research. We also have a memorial scholarship in her name awarded each year to a Lewisville High School senior.

Months after Jess had gone home, I was flipping through her Bible one day, and found a little note stuck in between the pages of Scripture. It said, "God, whether I get anything else done today, I want to make sure I spend time loving you and loving other people because that's what life is all about. I don't want to waste this day." She wrote that knowing she was sick. Those words summed her up as a person.

In fact, Jess's words have become such a tremendous message

that our family regularly draws from, we had little cards made up as a reminder. I keep one in my office; it's in a frame that houses her picture. I look at her beautiful smile from time to time and remember what a special person she really was.

Juli's Path in Life

Jess would have appreciated the fact that her illness did bring about some good—it brought Juli home. Juli's one-year walkabout as a flight attendant was because she wasn't ready to be tied down. A career or marriage wasn't something Juli wanted to be tethered to after college. She grew up talking about being a coach and a teacher, but those things had to happen on Juli's terms. Still, I had a feeling she would gravitate toward that career path. She played some basketball, but she ended up excelling at volleyball and running track in high school. I might be responsible for her competitive streak, but she would probably argue that point with you.

Whatever those terms were for Juli settling down, they were met after Jess passed away. She is now the girls' coordinator at her high school and coaches volleyball and track. She's been successful at both coaching and teaching. And she's a wonderful wife and mother. She married her husband Sean in 2013 and they have two little girls. I can't say that I was disappointed Juli stopped flying to strange places in the middle of the night. I hope Juli doesn't miss that life either, because I hope she's exactly where she wants to be.

James's Path in Life

My son James was a lot like me when he was younger. He played a little of everything—football, basketball, and baseball. He was talented enough to play baseball in college. A first baseman and left-handed batter, James started all four years. Even though James was a good baseball player, his passion was football. When he played in high school, his best ability was that he was adaptable. He found ways to be a good player, despite being smaller and slower than most of the team. Figuring out how to do that on your own is one step in becoming a coach.

Because James is so much like me, it's predictable that he went into teaching and coaching. He married Lindsey in 2016, who is also a coach. James is a great father to his son Crew.

2004, Ronnie and James during senior season.

He already knew he wanted to coach without me trying to direct him toward the family business. Without being too biased, I can say that James is a natural coach. He always has been assertive and an intense listener. He's a people person and instinctively knows how to reach kids. The main difference between my son and me is that James doesn't let things get him down. Juli and I tend to brood over things a little longer, but James can roll with the whatever is thrown his way.

James became a head coach and athletic director at an early age. He still calls me for advice, which makes me feel both good and relevant in his life. I had a unique opportunity that most coaches don't get to experience. I was supposed to open the season against James's team. Unfortunately, I had to retire early for health reasons, and we did not get a chance to play against each other. That would have been one for the memory book. We did get to coach together, just never got the opportunity to go against each other. Probably good for him, or maybe not, but I think Stephanie was a little relieved.

HUDDLE UP WITH TOM THOMPSON:
FRIENDSHIP BEYOND THE FIELD

I didn't have a relationship, per se, with Coach Gage the season I played for him. He was a coach and someone to be respected, *even though I am almost seven years older than he is.* It was only after football season, and my record-breaking kick, that I began a friendship with Ronnie.

After our year together, he had been offered a high school coaching position. Some of our discussions centered on the pros and cons of leaving his current position at Austin College. After he made the decision to leave, I introduced him to a friend of mine who helped him sell his home in Sherman. We began to talk more frequently and I asked him to speak about leadership at my church's men's group. Little by little, Ronnie Gage and I started to connect.

Ronnie became involved in an existing walk in honor of Jess and to raise funds to fight brain cancer. From the inception of the walk, Teresa and I have sponsored the walk's t-shirts and secured the involvement of our church. When he calls to discuss the next walk, every year I tell him, "Coach, as long as I am drawing breath, we are going to sponsor the shirts." Friends support each other, no matter what.

Then, there are events in my life where Ronnie will show up unexpectedly. He came to my son Jon Rawles's last football game of the 2018 season. I couldn't believe it! Ronnie had driven an hour from his house to get to the game, and I knew the next morning, he and Stephanie were leaving at five o'clock to go on a trip. After the game, Ronnie drove that hour back home, and I'm sure cheerfully got up to leave for the trip. It meant the world to me and to my son, and that's the kind of support he freely gives his friends.

True Friendship

I believe true friendship is where you *make a choice* to have a friend. You can tell if the friendship is substantive if your friend calls you for no other reason than to talk to you. Or maybe your friend might have done something special for you for no other reason than they wanted to do something nice for their friend. If someone takes the time to check on you—that is a sign of true friendship. For example, I have one friend I have phoned faithfully for nearly five decades on Fridays to touch base.

True friends have also gotten rarer as I have gotten older. As true friends, Ronnie and I love each other. When we speak, there is always laughter, and our conversation encompasses absolutely anything. Like the men of a certain age we are, Ronnie and I reminisce about the old days frequently. Sometimes we talk about my experience of being at Austin College to play football, since that was the launching pad for everything else we've experienced together.

Neither one of us planned to come into each other's life, but Ronnie and I are always there for each other, just a phone call or a surprise visit away. And speaking of happy surprises, today is a great day for you to call a few true friends and say hello!

6

A Career Spent Coaching

I have always been told and believed that good players make us good coaches. I have enjoyed the players I've had the opportunity to coach over the years. Each team was different, and I can remember so many players and plays. These memories are treasures. I always appreciated our player's commitment and I love every one of them.

After forty-two years of coaching, I often get asked if there is one story of a kid with exceptional talent or ability who's thrived under my coaching—one that stands out more than the others. There's never a good answer to that question because I have coached thousands of kids in so many different areas.

1996, Ronnie and his 1996 quarterback, Michael Odle.

I've primarily coached in areas of blue-collar schools. In my experience, working-class families are generally supportive and let you coach their kids the way you need to coach. In those situations, you coach hard and let them know you love them. I've also coached a lot of kids who come from one-parent families. Sometimes those situations can be more challenging, and I'm always reminded of how my coaches worked with me after my dad passed away.

Some Kids Will Always Stand Out

Even with all the kids I've coached through the years, one student's story does jump out at me. Chris transferred to Lewisville High School around 1994. The school he had come from had problems that had rubbed off on him. He lived with his mother and had a chip on his shoulder, but I never found out exactly what that chip was because he was as standoffish as they come. You couldn't get close to a boy like that. You had to chip away at his shell bit by bit. With him, and kids like that, you must get through their walls. They begin to trust you when they see you have their best interests at heart. When that happens, kids start excelling and begin to understand they are capable of great things, regardless of their past or current circumstances.

This young man let me in and played two great years for me. He was good enough to play for the Air Force Academy. I thought the military would give him the structure and discipline he needed to reach greater heights, but somehow it brought out his old tendencies of losing control of his quick temper. When Chris would go out with his Air Force buddies, they would get in bar fights. And this young man would be the one who stands up when he should back down. He was quick to defend what he thought was right. Sometimes it got him in trouble.

Whatever Chris had to prove to himself, it wasn't what the Air Force had in mind. He was released from the Academy and laid out a semester before going back to school in California. Losing his Air Force commission must have been a wake-up call for him, because he went on to finish his degree, dedicating his life to teaching and coaching.

One day out of the clear blue, Chris's mom called me to thank our coaching staff for what we did for her son. By never giving up on him, he had a compass—even if he got lost for a while. He had turned into such a tremendous young man, and his mother credited it to me, which was humbling to say the least.

Six months later I got a call from Chris's aunt. His mom had passed away from a brain aneurysm, and the aunt wanted to make sure I understood how important I was to her sister and nephew. I was told that young man wouldn't have made anything out of himself if it hadn't been for the support from me. But that's not entirely true; it was the leadership of all his coaches, not just me, that helped him. Once we broke through his thick shell, he listened to us, and he was able to take his abilities to the next level. The rest was his own decision to grow up.

Every year at coaching school, I see some of my players who have stood out just like Chris. We have an annual get-together at lunch for any of the coaches who played for us at one time or another. I've had as many as twenty and as few as eight attend this luncheon. The first one we had was in Fort Worth, and the largest attendance we'd had of former players. There are at least forty-five kids that I know of who played for me who are in the coaching business today. Chris was among those alumni. I just could tell how different and grown up he had become. He was, and is, a perfect example of one of the reasons I wanted to get into coaching.

It makes you feel good to see the positive impact you've had in someone's life. I take great pride in knowing their experience growing up and playing was a good one. I am honored they chose the path of becoming a coach. And I'm sure if you asked other coaches for their stories, you'd hear thousands just like Chris's. Every coach has a unique background that allows them to reach their players. I grew up without a dad, so sometimes I can help kids work through their problems using that lens. That help doesn't come in the form of sympathy. Too often hand-holding turns into a crutch that doesn't do anyone any good. You must be careful how you approach young people. Being too hard or too soft on a student can have unintended consequences.

2010, First year to coach together at Barbers Hill High School.

I have always been one who's never been afraid to stand up in front of my kids to tell them how much I love them and appreciate what they do. Not everyone could do what we ask them to do daily. We teach them that life is hard and easy is not an option. We demand a lot of effort from our players, and not everyone can do that. Yes, we teach them how to play a game, and it isn't always a fun game. Student athletes must work hard to distinguish themselves on the field. These kids work hard, and as adults we sometimes overlook their efforts. Aside from their studies, they are learning life skills, work ethics, values, integrity, character, commitment, dedication, hard work, and fortitude—all rolled into a single season. If as coaches we don't teach players those things, then we are not doing our jobs.

Coaching the Parents of Players

It's not always the young people we have to coach. Sometimes we have to coach their parents. Back in the old days, if a kid got in trouble at school, the first thing he would ask is, "You're not going to call my parents, are you?" Today, if a kid gets in trouble, the first thing they say is, "I'm going to call my mom or dad." Too many parents are trying to lay the path for their children, instead of letting their children forge their own trail. We also live in such a fast-paced world that both parents can't spend as much quality time with their kids as in years past, so some parents make up for this by buying their children's affections and unrealistically inflating their young egos. I also see parents jump in to make waves when they really haven't been around enough to know what is going on with their children. I'm sure that behavior makes them feel better for not being as present in their children's lives, but it only serves to muddy the waters. Fortunately, there are still many good parents that are supportive of kids and coaches. I have made so many friends that are parents of players I coached.

I had a dear friend who was a school supporter for several years, whose older son played linebacker for me. The son was starter on our 1993 state championship team, and his younger brother had a shot at being a future quarterback. Now, the younger brother wasn't a bad kid or athlete, but when his time arrived, we gave the starting position to a player who was better than he was. That soured the relationship between his dad and me for a long time. The father couldn't understand why his younger son wasn't our quarterback since his oldest son had been so successful. After all, the parents had invested a lot of time and energy in the booster club. They were tremendous people, and I was disappointed it had come to this.

I've always told parents that it doesn't matter what our relationship is or what your status is. Everything coaches do, *or should do*, is based on the kids and their performance. I'm not going to treat one athlete any differently than the other. I'm not going to play favorites because your mom is a teacher, or one of your parents spends more time or money supporting the program than another. The kids are going to earn their way themselves and be accountable for what they do. As I said earlier, easy is not an option.

The worst-case parents are those who are downright mean to their own children or to the coaching staff. The burden in their hearts that makes such parents verbally abusive to their children, their coaches, or referees must be weighty. I have had to run parents off the sidelines during practice. I tell them, "We don't allow anybody down on the field when we are working." I have also sat in on several closed-door meetings with parents who came in with an agenda. Half the time parents want to air out whatever concerns are weighing on their minds. I try to let them speak their piece before we get into a discussion. I always tell them we can agree to disagree but let's hear what you have to say. But there are always one or two who are unreasonable and won't allow you to do that. They have no tact, and abusive speech has no place on my office or field.

At this point in my career, I don't think my skin is as thick as it used to be, or maybe I just have a shorter fuse, but I don't have as much patience with some of those people as I did in my younger days. I don't know if that is a function of my age or the trend we're seeing in America today, but across the board, people aren't as polite or patient as they used to be. They are quick to speak and slow to think. It's like as a society we've overturned the whole basket of interpersonal skills. That scares me because the bad behavior of parents is passed on to their children.

I have to treat parents sometimes like I treat their kids. If an athlete knows you care, a coach can get after them. A coach can be demanding and set hard-to-achieve goals. With that combination, kids are not going to put up much opposition to that approach. Consistency is the key. You can't be up one day and down the next. They need to fight everyday with focus and determination.

It is the same with parents. It is hard for parents when their kid doesn't start or doesn't get much game time. It is hard for them to argue (although some of them will argue with a wall) when a coach tells you their role is different than what your expectations are. "Regardless of how you feel, somebody has to make that decision, and thank goodness that decision still falls on the coach's shoulders. Don't misunderstand the fact that we love your son, what he stands for, and the role he plays on the team." Coaching doesn't start, or end, with yelling and berating. Coaching starts and ends with love. If we all took that approach, everyone's life might be a little bit better.

HUDDLE UP WITH TOM THOMPSON:
THE IMPORTANCE OF SETTING AN EXAMPLE

In 2005, when I was teaching my MBA class in organizational behavior, I decided to share an idea with the students based on the "working for free" notion, which is finding areas in life where you can give back your time and talents, and it's not about the money.

Years ago, I heard a presentation that suggested people are happier when they have hobbies and when they volunteer, because it gives them a greater sense of purpose. That deeply resonated with me, and I've always told my students that they need to volunteer at *something*. Whether it be spending time at an animal shelter or at the Small Business Administration center mentoring other students, one should give something back to their community.

I've certainly seen the benefits of volunteering in my own life, and I've made it a point to continue to give back to the football community in the best way I know how—coaching.

Being a Kicking Coach

I love the game of football. I always have and hopefully always will. Currently, I am a volunteer kicking coach at Austin College. I say volunteer, but I get reimbursed for mileage and expenses. That doesn't quite count as a paid position, but I'd hate to misrepresent my place. Next season will be my tenth season as a volunteer coach, and I don't see any signs of stopping.

The dynamic of kickers on a football team is unique. We are an integral part of a football team, but we're also an island to ourselves, since the skills needed to be a good kicker don't translate to the rest of the positions. Distance and accuracy are numbers that any kicker can hang their helmet on, that no other position measures.

The overarching lesson for new kickers is they have to realize they are part of the team even if they are set apart. How do you teach that a kicker's performance is a team, rather than individual, measure? That's done by creating a team within a team. In other words, all of the kickers are taught to view themselves as each other's teammates.

That's where coaching makes a big difference. Of course, each player has to be able to read the field and the weather, and do the physical task of kicking the ball through the uprights, but there's a huge mental aspect to it as well. There are physical modalities as well as sports psychology techniques, such as mental imaging, where you continue to picture in your mind the outcome you are seeking.

Mental imaging is a concept primarily developed and based on sports psychology, and I coach all of my kickers using this principle. Great coaches use this same technique with their players, even when they're just beginning to get interested in sports, or are in pee-wee leagues, to help them set goals. You begin by painting a picture in your mind of an outcome you are seeking. In mental imaging, every time an athlete trains or exercises, he sees himself achieving the goal. But he is also setting himself up for dealing with the behavioral limitations.

If you haven't rehearsed yourself realizing a goal in your mind, you will be reactionary instead of proactive during the real-life goal-reaching process. You will not be in control of the events that need to happen and the limitations that must be overcome to achieve that goal, and therefore you won't know how to react when you do encounter an obstacle. It's the same with football as it is in daily life. We need to imagine ourselves succeeding all along the way to ensure we'll be ready to claim the victory when it is right in front of us.

Whether you realized it or not, the first time you heard *The Little Engine That Could,* you were introduced to mental imagining. As children, we learned through this example that if we first believed we could do something before we'd ever reached the goal, we would get there if we kept moving forward.

If you realize the way you view things or the way you react to adversity in achieving goals is an inhibitor, lay the groundwork with mental imagery before embarking on any goal. If you see yourself achieving your goal and recognizing the pitfalls before they happen, you will become more confident, and your old pessimism could just melt away.

While it's difficult to look forward to facing the obstacles that stand between you and your goals, remember to default back to the act of changing the way you think. You can still remain optimistic in the face of these adversities if you change your *can't* to a *can*!

7

Faith and Football

My family did not attend church together when I was growing up, but my mom would get up every Sunday and send us to Sunday school. We kids would go as told, but I never remember going to church with my parents. I'm not sure why they never attended. At that time, I never questioned it. I just did what I was told. I do know Mom was a baptized in a river in Oklahoma where she grew up, and she was a Christian. We used to go to family reunions and I remember everyone standing around the piano and singing hymns. My mom was part of a Christian family, and I know I'll get to see her again one day and get to thank her for her part in bringing me to Jesus. Either way, there was never a doubt about my mom and dad caring for us. They loved us and expected good things for their children.

When I was twelve years old, I got invited to go to a church camp in Arkansas. That invitation was a pretense to get me to play third base on the church's softball team. I guess you could say that sports have been the root of all things good in my life, and it was through that life-changing camp I found Jesus. I came back home and accepted Christ the very next Sunday.

My father had already passed away when I was baptized. Mom didn't attend the service when I came to the Lord, although I'm not

2009, Ronnie and Stephanie after his induction into THSCA Hall of Honor in 2009.

even sure I told her. It was an odd situation, but like many things in my life, that's just the way it was.

The Impact of Faith on My Life

I've been fortunate that Stephanie came from a solid Christian background. We've been able to create a Christian family, and we raised our children in a godly way. Going to church and being baptized on my own wasn't easy. It takes support to walk the way.

I call myself a Christian. I believe in God. I trust God. I have faith in God. But I am not sure I am always a good disciple of God. My relationship with God is still growing, as it should be. I don't think it is anywhere near where it needs to be, but I suspect it won't be perfect until I'm standing next to Him in the great hereafter. Until then, I can look to my family and friends and draw strength and lessons from them.

My daughter Juli has taught me so much about myself and life, so it's understandable that she would inadvertently give me a lesson on faith. Juli's husband Sean works in sales for the Dallas Cowboys organization and was thinking about taking a job in California. They were building a stadium out there for two teams. According to Sean, the job would be a boost to his career. Juli and Sean's daughter was a year-and-a-half old at the time, and we were devastated we'd be so far away from our granddaughter. Neither Stephanie nor I handled the situation well, because we put our needs before the welfare of my daughter's family.

When I realized what we were doing, I prayed one night for God's forgiveness. I needed to be a better father and less selfish. The *very next afternoon* I got a call from my daughter. She told us that Sean had backed out on the deal and they were going to stay in Dallas. There is no doubt in my mind that God intervened.

Living in God's light doesn't always mean getting the things you want. You don't always understand the things that are happening to and around you, but I know He is there. The Almighty has our best interests in mind—even if we don't. I trust the fact that He will continue to lead my life and I am going to be there with Him one day. I'm going to be there with Jess and everyone in my life that I've loved. Knowing that is worth all the mustard seeds of faith I've ever planted.

The Importance of Faith in Coaching

I honestly cannot imagine getting up every morning without leaning on the promises God has given me. I also can't understand how anyone could suit up and take the field without some sort of faith.

If I'm honest, my faith got stronger after my daughter passed away. It took me time to stop being mad. I couldn't understand why this had happened, but I realized that all I had to lean on was my faith. If we listen, God, the Ultimate Coach, can lead us through anything.

Faith is something I've tried to instill in our players. Even though Christianity and any public show of prayer has become taboo to some, I have never been afraid to pray with any of my players. I have prayed before and after every game that I have ever coached, at every school I have ever been. How ridiculous is it that in school that you can't sit down and pray as a group? I am not trying to teach a creed or cram dogma down their throats. If they don't feel like praying, they don't have to. If they don't want to listen to a message we give, they don't have to. I do believe we should respect everyone's beliefs and their religion. But I won't quit praying just because it makes some people uncomfortable.

2018, Daughter Julianne Penix coaching track at Arlington Heights High School

In fact, I extend those general lessons by talking to my athletes about the importance of faith and family. I always remind the kids to thank God for everything they've got and their families. "Go home and tell your mom and dad you love them and kiss them," is the most important thing I've ever coached my players on. Gratitude for what you have creates a humble heart and having a humble heart is the first step to having faith. People without faith, teams without faith, schools without faith…I imagine those people must live a lonely, miserable life.

I want to make sure my players know that I am a Christian and my faith is in God. I don't know how you make it without that. Plus, how could I hold my greatest treasure back from my players?

HUDDLE UP WITH TOM THOMPSON:
TAKING IT AND MAKING IT ON FAITH

In November of 2007, I was kicking back in my office when I first heard the name Mike Flynt. The story came over the internet about a Franklin, Tennessee, grandfather who played football for Sul Ross

University in the late 1960s and early '70s. He'd been kicked out of Sul Ross for fighting and never played his senior year, 1971. Flynt finished his credit hours at another college, but technically graduated from Sul Ross. Flash forward a couple of generations, and Flynt is at a Sul Ross reunion opining about missing playing his senior year.

"Stage a comeback," said Flynt's old roommate.

That's all it took. Mike Flynt, a retired fifty-nine-year-old and the inventor of the Powerbase Fitness exercise equipment, found out he was eligible to return to his alma mater. Flynt sold his house and moved back to Texas. He'd eventually get some game time and be the oldest recorded person to play in an NCAA game.

Huh, I thought. And that's all it took for the wheels to start turning.

I don't know about you, but I often have conversations with God inside my head. After reading Mike Flynt's story, the chat went something like this:

"God, I might have some eligibility left."

He said, "You should act on it."

Not Just Another Old Guy

As it turns out, it wouldn't be as easy as just filling out a few forms and suiting up. After Mike Flynt did what he did, the NCAA was deluged with old guys trying to get eligibility back to play. The NCAA already had their guard up, so to speak, when I started the process in December of 2007.

I didn't ask anybody how I should go about this. I simply went through what I thought would be the logical steps by first contacting the NCAA. I realized that Division III would be the only division I could go into because of my age. I then found out that the individual conferences oversee eligibility issues, not the NCAA. I would have to target a school in a specific conference to get the process going.

There were a few schools nearby, but I focused on Austin College. The school had a robust academic reputation that drew me to it. I emailed Austin's athletic director about my chances for eligibility and got a less than stellar response: "Thank you for your interest; however, the fact that you have a terminal degree means that most likely you don't have any eligibility remaining."

That didn't surprise me much. It was incredible to the NCAA that anybody could fall through the maze of rules they had to still have eligibility at my age and with my existing degrees. I'm sure they wanted to make it a nonissue for all the Mike Flynt wannabes, and I was initially declined.

Undeterred, I decided to take a more personal approach with a few phone calls, and went to Austin College in February 2008 for some meetings with administrators, and that's where I met Coach Gage. I received permission to apply for the following fall. I also found an ally in Tim Millerick, the vice-president of student affairs and athletic director. He pushed my cause all the way through the NCAA. It looked like I was going back to school, with or without eligibility to play.

Denied but Determined

I took it on faith that I would be able to get on the team. Camp was scheduled to start on a Sunday. That Friday before I got a call from Austin College's new assistant athletic director, David Norman, telling me my waiver had been denied. The NCAA wasn't agreeing with my presentation of the facts; the denial had nothing to do with my age.

I told my wife Teresa about the rejection. She started to quiz me about the rejection. Was that it? Could the decision be appealed?

Why don't you just go back to school and see what happens? She wasn't wrong. What could it hurt if I kept pushing a little and went back to school? There were appeals. There are always appeals, but I couldn't take advantage of that if I wasn't a student.

I kept moving forward and soon went to a football camp that I couldn't participate in. Coach Gage's solution to my unique problem was to make me a student coach. All that meant was I could dress up as a coach and stand on the sidelines during games. I would be a glorified fan on Saturdays. During practice, I carried an air horn. Every five minutes I'd blow it for segment change. That doesn't sound close to anything I wanted, but it was a step in the right direction. One of the requirements to letter at Austin College was two years of participation in a sport. Student coaching would count as a year of participation. I just had to hang on until the appeal come through.

The clock marched on to September, and still there was no word from the NCAA. I drove back and forth to college every day. My son Jon Rawles was a toddler at the time, and Teresa was working a full-time job. We had no time together and I was tired. I had such angst and frustration over the whole situation. In one of my conversations with God one morning, I boldly said, "Look, Nolan Ryan does not have to ask you to help him do what he does. You've got to give me some hope and help me here. Because if I am not supposed to do this, I want to go home and be a husband and a father."

After practice that very afternoon, I took a different path back to my car. I'm not sure what made me break from my routine, but I did. I kept hearing my name being called, but my hearing was starting not to be as good as it used to be, so I took another step. Then I thought, *No, turn around.* There was the athletic director. He had been calling after me and said, "I was looking for you. I spent the entire afternoon with the NCAA going over your situation."

Instantly my stomach pancaked to the sidewalk. I expected he wanted to give me the bad news in person, so I stood there silently as he continued. "I ended up reading the regulations line-by-line with the representative. We finished the last line and I said to the NCAA representative that it looks to me like this man has eligibility. Tom, the representative agreed."

The only words that formed on my lips were, "Oh, my gosh."

I almost didn't hear the athletic director over the blood rushing through my ears. He continued, "There's a catch. To fulfill the transfer clause, you have to participate for a year as an undergraduate. You're going to transfer into a grad program, and that is how you do that."

I can't honestly tell you if I would have given up or not that day. I don't think I would have, but I do know I could see God's hand at every step of the way, and that's what kept me going. He gave me the inspiration to start this process. He heard my prayer that day walking back to my car. He knew what my limits were, and exactly when to intervene.

How could anyone doubt there is a power in the Lord we call upon that is greater than our own? It's there and is as necessary a component to a good and successful life as food or air. As necessary as football in Texas.

8

Highlights Under the Bright Lights

If you're an athlete, you grow up talking about winning and being a champion. You don't play if you aren't looking to win. You have

1993, Poster that was made after 1993 State Championship game with Ronnie's picture under quote. This picture includes all his coaching accolades through 2004.

to plan your journey and go for it step for step. You have to understand what you want and why you want it. Everyone wants to make the key play at the state championship game. That's what the hours of physical conditioning and running plays are for—to win. Statistics and victories are all hallmarks of "winning," but there have been many accomplishments in my career that don't always fall in those categories. Coaching students like

Chris, who became a coach after leaving the Air Force Academy, would be one such win.

Career Highlights

My first head coaching job was at Northwest High School from 1987–90. When I took the job, the team had lost twenty-two of thirty games the three previous years, and was 0–10 the year before I arrived. But it wasn't just *one* bad season. The program had been down for some time. By my third year at Northwest, we made the playoffs for the first time in twenty-seven years. That accomplishment was a big deal to me. It wasn't winning a championship. To take a team that was at rock bottom and turn it around in a short period of time, that's something I've always been proud of.

After four seasons at Northwest, I went back to Lewisville in 1991 as the head coach. I wanted to keep the personal momentum up I had created at Northwest and let it flow through to my coaching at Lewisville. I always wanted to see where this profession would take me. I think I did a pretty good job of keeping the momentum and continuing to improve my career. The second season I was back at Lewisville, we were 10–2–1. We were beaten in the quarterfinals, but I was still proud of the team for their accomplishment. The next season, in 1993, the kids were hungry to get back in the limelight. They all worked so hard that year and it paid off. We made it all the way to the championship game—at the Astrodome.

Soon after we won the last game of the regular season, I received an encouraging letter on December 15, 1993, that was sent to me by a Lewisville High School teacher.

> *Dear Ronnie,*
> *I remember not too many years ago, I told you how won-*
> *derful it was for LHS to finally have a head football coach who*
> *demonstrated so much love and care and concern for the young*

men who came into his program. I know that it makes a man of strong moral character to dictate a very important code: love for a child must come BEFORE loving the win that is possible in a game of skill.

Again, I am moved to put to paper the feelings I experience when I see you hug Topher after making that field goal, when I watch every single Farmer football player hold hands as the coin is tossed, when I watch the other coaches express utter joy and jubilation when Zeb breaks up the opposing "big play," and when your voice cracks at the pep rallies as you praise the pride intrinsic in so very much of this school.

You are so very good for this student body, for this faculty, and for this community. I can only imagine what kind of grief you have to deal with each and every day when everybody wants to get "on the winning wagon" or tell you what you "ought" to do. Remember how important you are to so many people: your loving family, your assemblage of coaches, your faculty, and your players.

I can honestly say that I am very proud to associate myself with this high school and its Fighting Farmer football team. I remember days when I would hesitate to lay claim to that association. You are the reason for spreading so much positive assurance that youth can succeed if we only love and lead them.

May you have a safe trip to the Astrodome and may you, your family, the coaching staff and each and every member of the squad celebrate this very special opportunity!

Sincerely, Sally Tate

Her kind words were a reminder of all of the people who made our team so great. It wasn't just about the team and the coaching staff. Our teachers and parents and community were all behind us 100 percent. Still, the magnitude of what was about to happen didn't hit me until I saw Coach Wilson as we were loading up to head to Houston.

Coach Wilson was the district's athletic director and more importantly my greatest mentor. We met eye-to-eye the night before we left for Houston, and it dawned on me right then how big this was going to be. I was looking at a guy who never got the opportunity to play in a state championship game. I was about to go play in the biggest game of my life, and we may never get back to this place, ever. It hit me all of a sudden—*we've got to win this thing!* Coach Wilson and I looked at each other for a minute and teared up. We didn't have to say anything, and we knew exactly what the other was feeling. Thoughts of what we had accomplished and where we were headed soon became a reality. I had made it to the most elite game a high school coach can be a part of—the Texas High School State Championship. Wow!

1996, Ronnie and young James on sideline during 1996 State Championship game in Waco, Texas.

Sitting in the seats of the Astrodome, you get a fair sense of how big the enclosed field is. When you're on the sidelines inside, you feel like a flea in beach ball made of steel and turf. I was able to shake off that feeling, but most everything else was a blur. This was a dream come true. I was so nervous I left a coach and three players at the hotel we were staying in! I did not find out until after the game that they had been left behind and had to catch a ride from one of the parents. The game was one of the best state championship games ever played. It was back and forth from the first kickoff. The game literally came down to the very last play, and we scored with *twenty-seven seconds* on the clock. Our forty-three to thirty-seven win gave Lewisville their first state championship, ever.

At the whistle, the stadium darn near exploded with noise and energy. The level of emotion from the team, the parents, the coaching staff, and the residents of Lewisville can't be described. There was yelling, hugging, crying, and just about everything in between. That win was so monumental that the sense of community and pride felt in Lewisville is *still present* when someone "remembers when" they were at the game. It's like a legend being passed down around a campfire.

Now, I try not to be a boastful person and to me that game was great, but the legend didn't just happen at the Astrodome. The legend was created through all those practices and games leading up to the championship game. Those boys kept the faith and momentum up all season. The winning play with twenty-seven seconds left on the clock to clinch the 1993 State Championship was simply the icing on the cake.

This group of young men were determined and will always be remembered as the team that brought a championship to Lewisville. They finished the season with 15–0–1 record. We were the 5A division 1 state champions, which at that time was the highest division in Texas. Good things happen to good people, and those kids were special. They earned and deserved the final outcome.

As a coach, you've got to shake off big wins as much as you have to put

1993, Game face. Ready for another victory with the Lewisville Fighting Farmers.

tough losses behind you. Resting on your laurels only gets thorns in your backside, so you hit it hard again the very next day.

For the next several years, Lewisville continued to make it to the playoffs. In 1995, we felt like we had a team that could get back the state championship. We came up a little short, getting beat in the third round. That defeat stung as hard as any I have experienced on the field. There were seven seconds left in the game, and a kid kicked a forty-seven-yard field goal to beat us as the clock ran out. You had to admire the kick, but it sure broke our hearts.

You dust yourself off from those losses because there's nothing else to do but to forge ahead. People think coaches just remember the big wins, but the gut-wrenching losses can linger with you a long time. You don't have any choice but to move on. Like life, you have to trust what tomorrow will bring.

The 15-0 Team

In 1996, I had a group of kids and coaches that wasn't an overly talented group, but they were warriors. The thing about the 1996 team that just impressed me was we just got better and better and better as the season went on. I don't think we ever peaked as a team. Those kids fed off each other. The team dynamics were something beautiful, and I don't know if I've ever seen it before or since. They pushed and encouraged each other and were committed to being the best they could be. They had a chemistry and knowledge of the game that made my coaching job more about execution than teaching.

They went undefeated that season. Fifteen wins and not even a whiff of a loss. They were just a unique group of kids, and that was one of the most fun seasons I've ever coached. It didn't hurt matters that they went on to be state champions that year either.

So on a resume, those would be some of my career highlights.

However, I get way too much credit and recognition. I had coaches who could carry me on their shoulders. They were loyal and we truly cared about each other. When it was time to compete, our kids were prepared and we were going to play hard. That is all our kids knew because we demanded it. We had high expectations and we had fun working together toward the same goal.

In the big picture, an undefeated season and two state championships don't come close to the hundreds of wins I've had in coaching. I measure those in how the kids I've coached have gotten on with their lives. Every year I have dozens of former players that contact me, and that's what really matters most. It always comes back to the relationships that you treasure.

1996, Eric De Los Santos, Michael Odle, Luke Taylor, and Joey Longoria hold boxes of specially made Cheerios with a picture of the 1996 Fighting Farmers team on the box.

Players Who Became Coaches

Among the kids I've coached who've gone on to become coaches themselves, there are three in particular who have kept in touch regularly: Eric De Los Santos, Michael Odle, and Mike Phillips.

They've each had successful coaching careers and I'm proud to see the men they've become—men of character, coaches who aren't afraid to do things the right way and who genuinely care about their kids, their school, and the community.

Eric De Los Santos

I've known Coach Gage since high school, and I'm now thirty-nine years old, so that's long time, to say the least. Our relationship started as one of player–coach. I was just a role player on a team filled with stars. He never treated me or made me feel like a lesser athlete or piece of the puzzle. He helped me get into college. I probably would not have gone to school if it wasn't for his belief in me that I could not only go to college but play football and graduate as well.

I made it a point to always come by the school when I was home on break to visit with him and say hello. Once I graduated, he hired me as a middle school coach at Marshall Durham Middle School in Lewisville. It was a tremendous honor to work under him (even if it was just a middle school position). At this point in time, our relationship was very professional. It gave me an opportunity to just watch and learn from him and his staff that was second to none, in my opinion. As a young coach, all I wanted to do was learn as much as I could and not get on his bad side.

Once we both left Lewisville (Coach Gage to Austin College and me to Frisco Liberty) we began to talk more about non-football topics. He really began to mentor me as a professional, and more importantly, as a man. He's poured into me and my family over the last fifteen years or so. I cherish our relationship more now than ever.

My dad is very involved in my life and I love him like no other, but I truly cherish my relationship with Coach Gage. He's another father figure for me and I'm so grateful for his and Stephanie's guidance. So much so, I named my first son Gage (he's a pretty awesome kid too).

Coach Gage has really been a living example of professionalism. This profession is full of guys who feel like they've earned it so they don't need to pay it forward. He has never been that way and has always wanted to do right by kids, coaches, and the community. He's taught me to coach kids with high expectations but also to love them and care for them outside of athletics. I've taken that with me throughout my career. As an athlete he's always demanded our absolute best. He coached apathy and attitude more than Xs and Os.

I enjoy our time at the Texas High School Coaches Association, Coaching School every summer. We always meet up and walk around the exhibit and talk. Over the last five years, I along with about fifteen other coaches who once played for Coach Gage get together with him and his family and do a "Lunch with Coach" every year at Coaching School. It's really a great time for us to all reconnect before we get really busy again. It's turned into a pretty neat event. People who played for him at Northwest, Lewisville, Austin College, and Barbers Hill all show up. This past summer, we invited our wives to the event and that made it even more special.

Being a coach is the greatest fraternity and profession in the world. Every day you have an opportunity to make a real difference in people's lives. We have the responsibility of standing in the gap between what our society is pushing and the values that we know are tried and true. Commitment, trust, discipline, how to treat women, how to speak and act. The list goes on and on. Coaching is a platform to help mold young people into positive contributors in our communities. The crazy part is, it could be years before you realize you've actually made a difference, and because of that, this profession can be extremely exhausting. I wish I knew what it felt like to be a great coach; I don't think I've done it long enough to be great. But I can say with a shadow of a doubt, it's worth it! I've done this for seventeen years now and I can't imagine doing anything else.

The biggest reward I get from coaching is when former players stop by to say hello or send a text to see how things are going or thank you for helping them in some capacity. To me those types of actions speak louder than any score or trophy and are much more rewarding because you've made more than an impression, you've made an impact.

Obviously, we sacrifice a lot of time away from our families. Coaches tend to spend more time with other people's kids than they do with their own. But having a strong coach's wife who understands and can keep the family machine rolling is vital to being successful. There are many sacrifices, but the biggest to me is time away from my family. Thank God for Johnna (my wife), because she's been solid from day one.

Coach Gage has many positive qualities, and I've always admired how much he cherishes his wife and kids. I remember after games when I was in high school, his entire family would come on to the field. It didn't seem like a big deal at the time, but I know now how important a good coach's wife is to this profession. He's always been a husband and father first. That's a quality that I think any man in any profession should pray to have.

If you can't tell, I think the world of him. I love being around him and his family. He's got a such a genuine heart for people. He's handled situations with such grace and humility. His ability to inspire and demand all at the same time is a characteristic I wish I had. More than anything, I believe his greatest quality is his strength and belief in Christ.

Michael Odle

I met Coach Gage in 1992 while an I was an eighth grader at DeLay Middle School. Coach Gage coached me at Lewisville HS from 1993–96. After high school he remained my mentor, and I was still in contact with him and his family. I would coach under him as he was an athletic director for LISD, and then he hired me as his offensive coordinator at Barbers Hill in 2010.

He greatly impacted my life as an athlete. I learned valuable lessons under Gage's leadership that helped me grow into the man I am today. His will to compete and love his players brought us closer together and gave us the confidence to handle adversity both on and off the field.

When you put "Coach" in front of your name, it means so much more than the number on the scoreboard. Coach means you inspire the uninspirable, you fight for the program and the kids that come through it, you instill belief in athletes that they can do what seems impossible, it simply means you are always available when your kids need you.

We sacrifice every day for the sake of our players and programs. We signed up for this; we know the struggles that can come, and we also know that without struggle, there is no reward. It's a beautiful game that impacts so many people on a variety of levels. I do not know where I would be without sports or football; the game and my coaches have changed my life and given me opportunities that I could have never seen.

I have seen so many sides of Coach Gage and watched him triumph and watched him suffer. I have watched him coach, lead, and love his family. We have an unbreakable bond because of football that has grown into the game of life! I remember playing and working for Coach

Gage and my goal was to simply make him proud of me with my effort and determination of the task at hand.

I love the man. He gave me a chance when doubt was there. He gave me courage when I wasn't sure I could reach my goals. He gave me a chance to become a man by allowing me to use football as a platform to grow into the person I am today. Coach Gage is loyal, loving, and passionate about the things he loves. This goes for his life and in football.

As a coach, he lives through me each and every day. I am a reflection of the man, coach, mentor, father, and husband he is. I took notes of everything Coach Gage is, and I simply would not be who I am or where I am without Coach Ronnie Gage.

Mike Phillips

I met Coach Gage when I was fourteen years old, so I've known him for over thirty years now. I'd played sports for several years before I played for his teams, and you could tell right off the bat that he cared. The previous coaches from my former school, they weren't like him. And they weren't successful either. Coach Gage had a completely different mentality. He was emotional, and he wasn't afraid to cry in front of us. He would get himself so worked up but it was because he had such a passion for what he did and such a passion for us. We know he cared for all his players.

Northwest had a bad record and he took over when I was in eighth grade. My dad had been our coach from third to sixth grade. We had a pretty good group of kids who grew up together and really gelled together, and when we ended our freshman year, we hadn't lost a game. Our sophomore year we also had a winning record. Our junior year, we made playoffs for the first time in thirty-two years. In fact, my dad was a senior on the last team that competed in a playoff game at the same school.

I know from my personal experience that a coach can definitely make or break the team. When you have guys in charge of a group of young men, you know when they couldn't care less about the kids, are just there for themselves, and are trying to win and then get a better job. Coach Gage was not like them. He was there for us and the school he represented. You could tell that his main goal was to get the program turned around, but I didn't feel like it was to better his own resume.

He taught us about hard work and to not ever let someone tell us we weren't good enough. If he thought we were going to play someone and not win, we'd have never known it. We always practiced as though we were going to win. He had more confidence in us than we did, and he wanted us to be prepared for whatever was in front of us. Most kids that age don't have a clue what their future holds or what they want to do, but those are the years you're very impressionable and those are the same years your experiences begin to mold you into a young man.

Yes, we won two state championships in '93 and '96 when I was a coach in the Lewisville system, but playing for him those four years at Northwest, you'd have never known he had any other intention than to improve our program. The great staff he put together were all very similar to him in personality, and they all cared how they represented that school. They were a direct reflection of him. He did things right, even if it wasn't the popular opinion. He was able to build team unity because we knew from day one that he cared about us. He made it so comfortable, it was like we had a second dad. They had our complete trust. And it impacted me so much that in high school, I decided to become a coach, and I was a coach for fifteen years.

I had such a great experience growing up under my dad coaching and then Coach Gage, and I followed their examples when I was a coach. I did it the right way. I had kids from the first year I coached when I was twenty-six years old who still reach out to me, just like I still regularly keep in touch with Coach Gage all these years later. That goes to show you what type of relationship was built through Coach Gage and his coaching program.

In my opinion, a coach is someone who is a positive role model and influential in nothing but positive ways. A direct reflection of his school and the community. That's 100 percent Ronnie Gage.

HUDDLE UP WITH TOM THOMPSON:
MADE FOR THIS

For the 2008 football season, I was an undergrad student coach. That December I found out that I needed to have meniscus surgery on my non-kicking leg. I had the surgery but kept the proce-

1996, Ronnie and Stephanie celebrate State Championship win on sideline after game.

dure as secret as possible. There was no need to put a roadblock up when there didn't need to be one. If they would have told me, "Tom, there's no way you're going on because of your knee," I felt there would have been no reason for me to finish another degree. This phase of my education was a means to the end of football. But I was expected to make a full recovery, so I kept my focus on my rehabilitation.

I was cleared for spring football in 2009, and I was terrible when I came back. But I came back even more determined. Since the moment I had been accepted to the program, I treated Coach Gage like we treated coaches when I was in high school. You didn't talk to a coach unless he talked to you. Just because I am older than Coach Gage didn't mean I could just chit-chat with him. So I treated Coach Gage like I was a scared freshman and always with the utmost respect. I didn't languish around in his office when I had business with him. I was in and out. That's the way it was.

Coach Gage didn't engage me much either. That meant that whenever he spoke to me, it mattered. Coach Gage denies this conversation to this day, but I had been kicking badly that spring. One practice he came alongside of me and said, "You know, Tom, you're not very good."

I said, "Yes, sir, I know. It just means I've got a lot of work to do."

On another occasion, Coach Gage needled me with, "How old are you again?"

I told Coach Gage and he replied, "You're almost old enough to be looking for retirement homes, aren't you?"

"Yes, sir, I know I am."

We both kind of smiled and it was back to practice. I know Coach Gage was ribbing me with a purpose. I was one of his players, not a publicity stunt for the college. I was a dyed-in-the-wool player and I needed to step it up. That I did.

Training with a Purpose

I trained and kicked as much as I could throughout out the spring and summer. During the summer months, I was kicking up to seventy-five balls a day. Before the fall months, I had to get a pre-NCAA physical. I was having some difficulty with my quad on my kicking leg, and it was determined that I had torn my quadriceps. It was at the point where the injury was going to calcify over. If that happened, I would have had to have had surgery. There would have been no kicking, ever, if that happened.

I chanced taking a middle road of rehabbing the injury with physical therapy until camp started in August. I got to fall camp feeling as good as I could about having a potentially career-ending injury. But on the third day of camp, it happened. I was kicking and it felt like someone had taken a baseball bat and just whacked it across my thigh. There I was, pretty much with zero mobility in my leg.

It took more intensive physical therapy and two weeks without kicking to get back to where I *might* be able to practice. The season was already three weeks old when I was able to hit the practice field with the team. Even then, I wasn't assured my leg would hold out well enough to kick.

The mental rehab was as bad as the physical end. I started doubting my decisions and purpose for coming back to school. Through the pain I had one of my conversations with God and asked, "God, if you wanted me to do this, why am I having to struggle back up the mountain again?"

I sensed Him telling me, "I made you for this."

My mental side changed when I heard Him. I suspect He had been trying to tell me this since the summer, but this was the first time I heard Him so clearly.

With God, a loving family, and a team that truly did want me to succeed, I knew there must be a greater purpose for my circumstances. I quit feeling sorry for myself and realized that everything was going to be okay. If I just showed up and participated, things would turn around. I worked up to kicking five, then ten, then twenty-five balls in a day. Before I knew it, I was going to full practices.

I continued to operate in that framework. There was nothing more than classes, practice, and my home life. I went to games and did what I was supposed to do. Most importantly, I left it up to Him.

All of September and half of October, I was still in practice and improving. During a few pre-games in October, the extra point field goal team would kick. Coach Gage, every now and then, would let me get on the field and do a kick at the end of warmups. He told me flat out, "I am not giving you anything. You are going to earn it." He meant it, too. And by this time, I was all in.

The Big Moment

The hard work blurred the weeks together until it was mid-November, when we had come down to our season finale against Trinity University. We scored a touchdown in the second quarter and the extra point team began assembling on the sidelines. The process is so robotic. Everyone knows their jobs. When they're called in, the mental version of muscle memory kicks in. So when one of the assistant coaches came over to me and said, "Get out there and kick," I put my helmet on and walked out on the field with ten of my teammates.

No one in the stands probably realized I was taking the field, except for my family. I barely realized it myself. The cheers from the fans, music from the bands, and any other background noise was muffled through the padding in my helmet. I wasn't paying attention to that anyway. There was a football sitting on the ground that needed to be kicked through the goal post. The sum of my mental energy was focused on that solitary goal. Not all the paperwork I had to fill out and the appeals to even be here. Not all the months of injuries I'd worked through. Or all the miles I drove to class and back, taking time away from my family. None of that mattered in this moment. There was only a ball and a goal.

I've heard that the human brain is like a giant calculator. In milliseconds, mine calculated wind speed, angular momentum, turf resistance, friction coefficients, velocity, then—BAM! The ball was up and through the goal posts before I knew what was happening. In the moments just before I kicked, the entire stadium had clued in that it was me, and when the point was good, they went World Cup soccer fan wild. I had just become the oldest person to score in an NCAA game at the age of sixty-one.

As great as my accomplishment was on that November day, my team still lost forty-four to ten. I executed my job, but my first loyalty was to my team, and I still feel bad about that loss. No matter what laurels we wear individually, it's how well the team does that matters. But I do know that it was pretty incredible to have played on Austin College's team. It truly was a dream come true.

9

Lessons from the Field

If there is one lesson that ties up all of my experience with athletics, from playing to coaching, it's work ethic. When I was a player, my coaches pushed hard and worked me even harder. I wasn't given much sympathy for being tired. There was no "not feeling like" going to practice. My coaches were as committed to the task at hand as I was.

I felt like they genuinely cared about us. They were always consistent in their approach to motivate and push us. There was no phoniness about them, and it was clear their goal was to make us the best athletes and young men we could be. It doesn't matter how

1992, On sideline with my best friend and defensive coordinator for many years, Terry Goode.

many skills go into making those individual components happen; if you don't have the work ethic to implement those changes, nothing will change. If you look at most successful people, I think you will see a strong commitment to hard work and perseverance.

I've tried to emulate those lessons in my own coaching. The legacy I hope to leave with anyone I've coached is being the best person you can be. It's not about being better than your neighbor or someone on TV; it's about being better today than you were the day before. If you can wake up and be a slightly better person than you were the day before, that's an accomplishment.

The Importance of Encouragement in Kids' Sports

While many kids have succeeded with good coaching, others don't have the fundamentals of character necessary to grasp that lesson. They hide behind their problems and use those as an excuse for anything that doesn't suit them. Many kids use their home life as an excuse, and rightfully so with some. I'm probably not as patient with justifications for not giving your all to yourself and your team, simply because of what I went through as a kid when I lost my dad. I believe that if you listen to your coaches and do what's asked of you, regardless of what's going on off the field, you can be successful on the field. It all comes down to players making the choice of what they want to make of themselves. At times young people don't even know they have a choice to make their lives better. Making good choices is not always easy, but again, easy is not an option.

I try to be there for kids who are at the crossroads and give them direction. Everyone, from the school counselor to the principal, can sympathize with any problem a young person might have. But someone has to motivate them to get up and do something with their lives. Although many have become coaches, most of my players won't find their life's ambitions on the football field. But that's okay. My job isn't to create an army of footballers for the next generation. My job is to inspire these kids to become great in their own way by showing them they can achieve more than they could imagine.

If you constantly tell a kid he's clumsy or slow, he'll never believe he's agile and fast. It doesn't matter if he aces every drill and smokes the rest of the team on the forty-yard dash. That young man will believe himself to be slow and awkward. On the other hand, if you encourage a middle-of-the-road player, he'll feel like he's a champion. You must build pride in the ability of a young man and the way he goes about reaching his potential.

1996, Ronnie, Julianne, and James after 1996 State Championship win. All wet from Gatorade.

Encouragement doesn't mean overinflating a young man's abilities. Encouragement lets him know that his hard work is being noticed. When you know someone is watching your development, you try harder. When you try harder, you do things you never thought were possible. That's a fundamental principle of coaching that should never go away. Young people need to know where they stand and how to get better. That's the only way any of us can thrive.

The Importance of Chemistry and Teamwork on the Field

I used to get asked every year from reporters or fans, "Coach, how is the year looking? How are things going to be?"

My response was, "I'll get back to you on that. I don't know until I see the chemistry of the team."

The chemistry of the team decides how a group grows together and how committed they are to be the best they can be. That connection will get everyone on the same page without much effort, and everybody will be pulling on the same side of the rope. Most importantly, the proper team chemistry means individual team members believe in the team's overall success. When individuals would rather play for the glory of the team than their individual stats, you've got the kind of chemistry that makes champions.

In the spring before the 1996 season, I was interviewing for a job in another large school district. The job would have been a great opportunity for me. I'd made it through the first two rounds and was asked back for a third interview. At that point, I got cold feet and backed out. When I was asked by a reporter why I didn't go for that final interview, I told him, "I don't know. There is just something special about this group of kids. I've just got a good feeling about them."

The 1996 Lewisville team wasn't loaded with Division I–level athletes. I called them "backyard players" who grew up playing the game. They enjoyed each other and worked extremely hard. The chemistry was just so tight that I had a good enough feeling about them to tank an interview with a larger program. What a premonition it was!

All of that led to an undefeated state championship season. I feel like we were still getting better in week fifteen. You would have thought there would have been quite a few Division I players out of that group, but I only had one kid who went on to play football at the Division I level. It wasn't the individual excellence that made that team. What created that undefeated season was how the individuals worked together. The chemistry was strong, and the leadership was solid in so many places. They believed in each other and what we were doing. They learned how to ride the momentum they created each week. They simply bought in 100 percent. That's an unstoppable combination.

What It Means to Be a Good Leader

Chemistry doesn't mean much if there's no one mixing all the individual chemicals together. That's where leadership comes in. From coaching to being the president of a company, all leadership comes down to finding a way to make people buy in and follow your direction. All of the leadership books and courses can be distilled down to that. There are tactics and techniques that you can employ to make that easier, but individuals have leadership triggers that speak to them. One kid might respond to praise, while another needs to be gotten onto a bit with some tough love for them to excel.

The price of leadership is usually born from finding those triggers. There's a toll in a leader's time and emotions that comes from learning about his people, but you have to become invested in their lives and stories to find out what makes someone tick. Then you wind them up and let them run. If you can't do that for the individuals on your team, you're not a good leader. If you're not a good leader, you shouldn't expect success to come your way.

Learning from Mistakes and Learning How to Handle Disappointment as Well as Success

Being a good leader doesn't mean that you won't make mistakes. Good leaders keep trying different approaches, and some of those are bound to fail. I don't believe you should subsidize your beliefs in order to hang on to kids. I think when kids prove that they don't want to be a part of what you are trying to do, you must look at other alternatives.

It has always bothered me when I lost a kid or two during the season. I've always looked back and asked, what could I have done differently? If there is something I can learn from that situation, I'll make changes where I can. But I can't spend too much time wondering where I could have made changes, because I have a team to lead forward.

For a coach, learning from your mistakes means being able to shake off losses and learn from them objectively. People talk about the big wins, but it is the tough losses that grind at you and you learn the most from.

When you quit learning, it is time to get out. If you don't get out, you replay the games time and time again, dissecting what you could have done differently to win. Coach Wilson told me one time, "There's nothing like the wins and there's nothing like the losses." You wake up on a Saturday after a win and you've got a smile on your face. A Saturday morning after a tough loss and you are intensely demoralized. There never was a bigger truth than Wilson's message of learning how to deal with both success and failure.

That is the beauty of athletics. A tough loss is not a good time to start chewing on kids. It doesn't matter whether the team played good or bad, you've got to be right there with them, in the middle of the disappointment. You've got to share the pain with them. Once they see you're hurting as badly as they are, everyone wants to build themselves back up later throughout the week. The lesson for young people is that winning doesn't always mean success and losing isn't always a failure. I have coached teams that weren't as successful but did everything they could do to win. They never gave up and always played hard. How can you not be proud of those kids?

*2000, Family celebrates Battle of Ax game win
against rival Marcus High School.*

It's Okay to Have Fun

Understanding wins and losses is key to another "Gageism," as my friends and family call my spurts of wisdom. "Work hard. Play hard. Have fun." Whether it is in practice or during a team meeting, you've got to find something to break up the monotony for a few minutes to have fun. This isn't to say that fun can't be hard work too. There is a fine line between working hard and having fun while working.

Another Gageism is: "Fun comes in winning and winning comes in hard work. It all goes together." I wish I had a formula to tell you how that works. It's more of a mindset than a rulebook when finding ways to bring fun into the rigorous physical work.

Lessons I Hope to Teach Others

To me, success isn't about just the wins and losses. It is about the things you learn and gain growing up as a young man in athletics. Hopefully, the kids I've coached will look back on that and realize that lesson. At the time, I know it is important to win and lose. But that's one of the things about coaching that you must overcome—the fact that there is so much emphasis on winning.

People don't stop to realize we are not like a college or a pro team, where we can go out and pick our team or recruit our team. You take what you've got and you develop them each year. If you have an injury here or there, you may not have a bucket to go pull something out of. But if you invest in your players and focus on their strengths, you'll be pleasantly surprised at just how perfectly the team can come together as one.

HUDDLE UP WITH TOM THOMPSON:
THE KICKER WHO NEVER PLAYED

Learning from mistakes, winning, losing, and having fun all hinge on teachability. The word sounds made up, but it's the marriage of learning and adaptability. If you're not open to learning and committed to applying that new knowledge, you're never going to grow at anything.

I emphasize the importance of teachability with every new kicker that comes in. I don't care how talented a kicker is at the beginning of the process. Their success will be determined by their ability to be taught. What my kickers learn, after having spent a year with me, is that I was right. The process I have in place for them can be tedious and boring at times, but the training pays dividends. If one is willing to embrace the process instead of constantly looking at the outcome, success is almost assured, even if it doesn't include game time.

The Insurance Policy

Ethan was one of my kickers who spent four years coming to

practice, although he never played in a game. He traveled with the team for a year or two because he oversaw the boards. If you're not familiar with "the boards," you will see two guys on the sidelines holding up boards with different pictures. These images alert the defense to which scheme they want to use without hollering and alerting the other team. The pictures might be of Tom Brady, a tiger, or even a moose. Each icon has a meaning that only team members know.

The guys in charge of the boards are usually injured players or a player that's not going to be in the game. Traveling with the team is the first step on the ladder to playing, and Ethan was ringing that bell.

By the time Ethan was a junior, he was an insurance policy if whoever was the kicker got hurt. Even though he never played a single game, he became a better kicker.

When it was all over, I asked Ethan, "Would you do this again?"

"In a heartbeat," he said with a smile.

Why would a young man practice with a team for four years never to play and still do it all over again? Who in their right mind would hold up boards on the sidelines just for the chance of getting in the game? Ethan would.

He understood that he might not have been good enough to play, but he was good enough to be taught how to kick better. He kept honing his skills because he was invested in the process—not the outcome. Sure, some people would say that Ethan failed because he didn't play and that he was crazy for sticking around for all four years. But that's not true. Ethan succeeded because he allowed himself to be taught and became better because of it.

Teachability Will Take You Far

Teachability is a key requirement to success, and almost no one teaches it. But I would rather coach a person with a high level of teachability and a low level of ability rather than a rock star. The highly teachable person can grow with a coach or a mentor and exceed someone with natural talent.

Another example would be how many people want to have a personal trainer but are not willing to be trained. They just want to say they have a trainer for the sake of their ego. Those people aren't interested in enhancing their level of fitness or living a long life.

People must adjust their definitions of success in order to be truly successful. Ethan was successful because he was willing to take the steps toward the goal of getting game time. He was able to travel with his teammates and build experiences he'd otherwise never have had. Ethan pushed his mind and body in practice to learn discipline that would transfer into his life later.

Since then, Ethan has made a comfortable life for himself and he's happy. Was my influence a part of him building a good life? I hope it was. All I know is that he invested in himself and reaped all the rewards teachability brings.

10

Change through the Years

A few years ago, I was invited to speak at a seminar. After I spoke, there was a Q and A forum for the company's directors and supervisors. The first comment I received was, "Well, coach , it must be really hard because the kids are changing so much."

My response was, "No, it's not the kids who are changing; it is the demands that we are putting on the kids that are changing." In addition to newer and harder demands, it seems parenting styles have shifted over the generations.

How School Athletics Has Changed over the Years

There is nothing fundamentally different about children today versus thirty years, or even eighty years ago. Kids will still do what you ask of them. They still want to be disciplined. They still want to be loved. They still want to be successful. Coaches may have to work harder to get all of

2004, City of Lewisville Citizen of the year. Very prestigious honor.

that done, but kids still need and desire those things. It is our job to find the method that is going to get that done. The difference now, versus forty-two years ago when I started coaching, is that it's harder to find the formula that is going to make that work.

There are hundreds of reasons for that change, from different family structures to the internet use. For the kids who want to be athletes, and who truly want to excel, the biggest change has come from parents and school districts.

The focus of athletics when I was younger was about having fun. You played hard with your friends, and the group pushed each other to be better. Now there are summer leagues, off-season programs, travel teams, and private classes and clubs for athletics that make athletics a full-time job for kids and parents.

Winning was just as important back in the day as it is today. However, kids are pressured into performing year-round to look for an edge, or by parents hoping to enhance their chance of a scholarship. Those conditions create opportunities to learn potentially bad habits and to have unrealistic expectations that can hamper any young person's growth.

That's why I've always loved off-season programs. I enjoyed the challenge of building a team and watching kids develop and mature. In the summer, kids should have some time off from sports and school to just be kids. Spending time with your family on vacation and working a job are experiences all young people should be able to have during their time off from school. During the summer, we run strength and conditioning programs. I always cut ours short a week or two, which was different from most other programs. Again, kids need some time to be kids, and they need to reboot and get ready for the grind of a new season.

We do a variety of activities during the off-season to keep the program fresh: competition days, relay races, and hundreds of other creative ideas to break the monotony of drill work and weight lifting. Our kids loved the variety. When that bell rings at the end of the school day, they hustle to get dressed knowing that we are going to get some quality work done.

2017, Football scrimmage between father's and son's teams

Breaks Make a Team Better

Your teams are built in those winter and spring months. During the breaks you'll see what your team is made of. You find out where your leadership is. You find out where your strengths and weaknesses are. You develop your work ethic. Our teams did not play hard by chance. It was because of the demands we put on them to work at a high level all the time. You teach your kids to recognize the importance of strength and conditioning and understand they are not just there for the glory of being on the team. Negative attitudes and behaviors can be addressed during the off season long before those things make it to the field.

This is the essence of coaching to me—making young people better versions of themselves. I don't think you have to have a long list of rules to instill self-governance in kids. Discipline is built on a foundation of expectations you present, and the consistency of standing by those expectations.

I'd like to say that every day of my coaching career has been a delightful experience, but some days you drag on. After recently retiring with forty-two years of coaching under my belt, I can honestly say if I had to start over tomorrow, I wouldn't change a thing. I've loved every second of it. There are negatives to everything you must deal with, but I would say overall that most everything I have gotten to do over the past forty-two years has been a positive.

My passion for coaching has always remained strong. I am so proud to be called Coach. When you look over a room of coaches, you see character and integrity written all over it. This is the greatest profession in the world, and I get a chance to make an impact each and every day. I hope that somewhere, some way, somehow I have made a difference. That is the legacy I want to leave behind.

1996, Celebrating with Neal Wilson and family after 1996 State Championship win.

HUDDLE UP WITH TOM THOMPSON:
CONNECTING WITH YOUNGER GENERATIONS

Coach Gage and I grew up in a different world than we live in today. Our role models were from the greatest generation. Many had seen the horrors of combat in Europe and the Pacific theater during the Second World War. Those who stayed stateside during those years suffered through rationing, took jobs that supported the war effort, and fought scrap drives. During World War II, the United States government encouraged the American people to participate in scrap drives. Citizens were asked to turn over to the government items that would prove to be useful in the war effort, but many of these items were also essential to surviving and maintaining a home. On top of that, those same men and women were touched in some way by the Great Depression. Scarcity, sacrifice, and service were the hallmarks of their existence. Those lessons were passed down to men like Ronnie and me on the football field.

Since the days of yore when I was in high school, the world has shifted three times—Watergate, Columbine, and September 11. Where there once was trust in authority figures, now there is skepticism. Schools and office buildings that were once safe public places are now places to fear. Our children conduct active shooter drills while live streaming. The social media fishbowl young people live in today creates a need to stand out from the crowd, while still hoping they make it home from school. Yes, the world has moved on since the world was as black and white as a John Wayne western.

Everyone Has a Story

The result for high school and college athletics is that kids are more concerned with themselves than they are with the team. In the old days, a win or loss for the team was the bellwether metric. Now, scholarships and superstardom reign supreme on the football fields and basketball courts of America. This, coupled with parents who reinforce the uniqueness of their children above all other factors, makes the first step of coaching that of teaching what and why teams are important. Kids look inward so often now, there isn't much of a frame of reference for teamwork.

The changing of the times can easily be seen in college football. Transfers from college to college were unheard of twenty years ago. Now, transferring schools is the norm. College football is a rearview mirror look at professional football. The self-interest in free agency comes before loyalty to one's team, but there must be a balance between individual achievement and team loyalty if any group is to excel. To strike that balance, you must look outside your frame of reference and do your best to understand young people today.

For anyone north of forty, putting social blinders on is easy. We shake our fists at the sky and mentally yell, *Darned millennials!* If you're as old as I am, you remember when rock and roll was going to dismantle Western civilization. Then it was "those dang video games." The list goes on and on. The last time I checked, the world is still running. Every generation has seen the ones who have come after as being softer and more scandalous than "our generation." The truth is kids are different with each generation, but they're also just the same—no better or worse than you were growing up. We get to see the extremes now more easily than before because we've become so much wiser with age.

We must open our hearts and our minds to the realities of young people if we are to be effective leaders. That goes for anyone who is outside our frame of reference. Does it hurt anything to listen and to ask questions of someone whose story is different than yours? How are we to minister to the world if we can't understand plights we've never considered? There's always a way to connect with kids if you simply listen.

11

The Day Everything Changed

It was a pretty normal Sunday morning in April 2018. We were getting ready to go to church, and I had what I thought was just bad indigestion. I took an antacid, hoping it'd ease the discomfort, but it just got worse and worse. I hated to miss church over a bit of heartburn, but after a while, I just couldn't stand it anymore so we went to the emergency room.

Stephanie and I never really talked about what might be going on. We were just doing our best to deal with it. She's a retired RN, so she's used to dealing with people not knowing what their bodies are doing to them. I tried to stay as calm as I could, for her sake as much as mine, but it did cross my mind that I could be experiencing the onset of a heart attack.

When we got there, they took me back to a normal-looking hospital examination room. It smelled like disinfectant, and machines were beeping all around me. They did a cardiac enzyme test, and the first one came back negative. They seemed worried still, so they kept me for observation and did another test a few hours later. I thank God that they did, because the second test showed the cardiac enzymes were rising, and they kept going up as the day went

BEST OF THE BEST IS WHAT WE STRIVE TO BE AND A LEGACY IS WHAT WE ARE TRYING TO LEAVE....

Northwest High School '87 - '90
Lewisville High School '91 - '05
Austin College '06 - '09
Barbers Hill High School '10
Paradise High School '10 - Pre...

2017, Picture of Ronnie sitting alone on sideline bench after James coached a playoff game. It is in the Fighting Farmer stadium where Ronnie coached.

on. Finally they determined I'd had a mild heart attack and admitted me to the hospital.

The Heart Attack

The news didn't really sink in when they told me. I remember just accepting it like it was any other piece of information. All that would change a few hours later.

When I'd been moved to my own room, the staff were still trying to figure out if my chest pain was heart-related or pulmonary or GI-related. If it was my heart, a nitroglycerin pill would get rid of some of the chest pain. So I took the pill, but after about twenty seconds, everything started crashing. My pulse was dropping. My blood pressure was steadily declining. Eight or nine nurses were scrambling around me. Stephanie's composure broke, and I could see the panic written on her face, even as she barked orders to the nurses who were working on me. "You better not let anything happen to him!" she shouted to the room full of nurses.

When you're a football coach, *you* call the plays. Right then, lying in that hospital bed, seeing a crash cart being rolled in, and feeling cold paddles against my chest, I realized how little control I had. Everything was happening around me, and I could do nothing to stop it. That's when I finally understood that this could be it. For the first time in my life, I was truly afraid. I was trying not to pass out; I was terrified that if I closed my eyes, I'd never open them again.

After many tense moments, they got everything back under control with medications. The pill did help my chest pain, so that meant it was my heart. We hadn't told the kids what was going on yet, because everything had happened so quickly, so we called them that night.

The next day, a cardiac catheter test determined I needed quadruple bypass surgery. Our kids were at the hospital for the cardiac catheterization and heard the results from the cardiologist. Open heart surgery was scheduled for the next day, and I had all my family and many friends in the surgery waiting room anxious to hear results.

The surgery itself didn't seem that bad; I remember going into the room and then waking up in a bed. I was in the hospital and was doing well. Of course, I had some pain but it was manageable. I was even up and walking in the halls on the day after surgery. Everything else went all right until the next Saturday, when I went into atrial fibrillation while the therapist had me walking. They had to readjust my medication and kept me an extra day for observation. Soon everything was under control again, my heart was beating regularly, and I got to go home the next day.

I'm also certain that as easy as it was for me to go to sleep for surgery and wake up with a fixed heart, my family, especially my wife, had to have struggled with immense stress and uncertainty during that process.

Community Support

Stephanie stayed with me at the hospital the whole time. She even slept there with me every night. I've been blessed with a strong family, and they were with me every step of the way.

I had quite a few people come in to see me. Friends and players came in, all wishing me well. It was like homecoming! All the coaches I'd worked with years came to visit. It even got to the point where the nurses were becoming concerned for my health; you don't think about it, but when you've got people there, you feel like you have to talk and stay awake. My body had just survived a heart attack and open-heart surgery and was trying to heal.

Even still, the reaction from my community reminded me of what happened when Jess passed. The outpouring of support we received made me appreciate how many people are genuinely concerned and cared about us.

I felt lucky. I wasn't in the ground, and the people who love me were right there beside me. I always felt God's presence during this time, and this reassured me that it was in His plan for me to stay around for a while longer.

2007, Family picture after game at Austin College.

HUDDLE UP WITH TOM THOMPSON:
THE IMPORTANCE OF FITNESS AT ANY AGE

If your body fails, no matter what you want to do or could do, you are not going to reach your goals. Although Coach Gage keeps himself in good physical condition, the importance of staying fit is illustrated by his heart attack. Ronnie might not have survived that ordeal had he not been in shape. The benefits of staying fit at any age go far beyond the day-to-day improvements we see in our lives. Staying fit reduces the recovery time for illnesses and lessens your chances for other debilitating conditions.

Fit for Life

You don't have to train for a marathon in order to get fit. Plus, our society often has it all wrong when it comes to ideas of what "fit" really means or what it looks like. The meaning of the original Greek word for *fit* isn't "ripped," "shredded," or "ultramarathoner." It's "useful." Therefore, the more fit you are, not only are you useful to yourself, but you are useful to other people. That logic runs away from the "me" side of personal fitness, but the more useful you are to other people, the more involved you will be in the world around you. So, you will be more useful to your family, church, company, and yourself if you are physically fit.

We all can make good choices that can impact our health. The question is will we make ourselves enough of a priority to do so? The biggest excuse for not exercising, or even eating right, is that there's no time. What we're really saying is that we are putting other responsibilities above our health needs. Children, careers, church, and any other area of importance will benefit from you being a fitter person. Aside from longevity, having a higher level of energy to participate in a broader range of activities benefits everyone else in your life, too.

Ten Minutes Makes a Difference

If fitness isn't something that has been a priority in your life, you can make a ten-minute choice to correct that. If you commit to ten minutes of physical activity every day, you'll be on the road to better health. If you keep building on that ten minutes of activity, you'll find that you want to do more. You will push yourself into different fitness goals because you feel better about yourself and you'll want to feel even better.

And all it takes is ten minutes. You have that don't you?

In my previous book, *Get a Kick out of Life: Expect the Best of Your Body, Mind, and Soul at Any Age* (Clovercroft, 2017), I shared that the ten-minute method is a primer for exercise or any area of your life that you want to change. Most people can do anything for ten minutes at a time, including fitness.

If you haven't had an exercise routine or you are not accustomed to exercising regularly, beginning the process can feel daunting. You might feel like you have to go from zero to sixty in a matter of a week in order to really see a change. But that mindset is not only false—it's dangerous. Apart from the injuries that can be sustained by overworking the body and not having knowledge about the weight room equipment, another major reason to take it easy is to make sure you can sustain the consistent effort.

Data indicates that most people who join a gym, even though they have the best intentions, quit around eight weeks later. This is an extremely prevalent phenomenon around January of each year. But if you stay consistent and keep to a ten-minute routine at the beginning, slowly working your way up from there, you'll have a far better chance of sticking with it and seeing results.

When you begin an exercise routine, go to a gym and pick any cardiovascular exercise machine that appeals to you. It can be a treadmill, a seated rowing machine, a recumbent bike—it does not matter which machine you pick. Get on the machine, dial the settings to the lowest level, and be active while getting your heart rate up for ten minutes. Then you stop, leave the fitness center, and you go home. If you can't make it to a gym, walk around your neighborhood instead, making sure your heart rate is elevated enough to begin to break a sweat.

Do these ten-minute workouts for *two weeks straight*. At the end of the first two weeks, start adding a minute to the workout as you feel comfortable. When you reach the thirty-minute mark, hold there for two weeks. Then you can begin to slowly introduce strength equipment into the routine.

While it may not seem like much to work out for a mere ten minutes, it's far better than doing nothing, especially if you have a sedentary job. So give it a try! Stick with it, find activities you enjoy doing, and begin to create a healthier lifestyle starting today.

12

A Hard Decision

After the surgery, the seven-day hospital stay felt like it dragged on forever. My mind was restless. I kept thinking about all the things I needed to do. *When am I going to get back to coaching? Am I going to be able to get back in time for two-a-days?* The questions came faster than I could keep track of them and I didn't have any answers.

After days of these unanswered questions running laps inside my head, I realized that *someone* might be trying to tell me something. I thought about it. I prayed about it. We had talked about my possible retirement even before the surgery, but I just could not pull the trigger. To be quite honest, I don't know when I would have retired had it not been for the surgery. That was the wake-up call. When I'd finally made up my mind, I looked at Stephanie and told her, "I think it's time."

That decision was solidified as soon as I was released. I had pneumonia in one lung after I got out of the hospital, which finally cleared up. But the hot air outside was scratching its way down my throat. I was coughing a lot, and I wasn't able to talk for very long without getting winded.

I knew I couldn't run practices. I was in no shape to even stand

STAFF PHOTO/MARGARET LEVERENZ

Lewisville head coach Ronnie Gage, right, discusses strategy with defensive back coach Billy Mitchell during the Farmers' 35-13 win over Duncanville.

Gage thanks community, team for 1996's 15-0 dream season

Reflecting back on this past season I realize just how fortunate I am to work at a school that is so rich in tradition. I am supported by a community that recognizes hard work and appreciates the efforts of our kids and coaches. I work with an administrative staff that is superior and loves kids. I work in a school that has a fantastic student body. The term "Farmer Pride" is a true reflection of what our school is all about. Realizing this, it's time to say thanks to so many of you.

I want to thank the community of Lewisville for your show of support all year. The turnout Saturday the 14th in Waco was tremendous and you played such a big part in that win and the success of our season.

I want to thank Mr. Killough, his staff and the wonderful faculty we have at L.H.S. You are all so supportive and understanding. None of you gets the credit you deserve for the job you do for our students. You're great!

I want to thank our student body, whose enthusiasm was phenomenal. I'm so proud of all of you. Farmer Pride was at its best in Waco last Saturday.

I want to thank Neal Wilson, Rody Durham and Linda Baker for being the foundation this program is built on.

I want to thank my coaches for doing the job I get too much credit for. I am so fortunate to

have each of you. Your loyalty and hard work is appreciated. You are professionals in every sense of the word. Our kids are fortunate to have you.

Finally, I would like to thank the 1996 Fighting Farmer football team. You taught me that you can't judge a book by its cover and that there are still such things as teamwork, heart, commitment and determination. The enthusiasm and efforts you gave for 15 weeks will always be remembered. I love each one of you and thank you for the season we had. You will go down as one of the greatest "teams" in the history of Texas High School Football. Your run to the championship was unbelievable. I am so proud of you and always will be.

There is such a thing as Santa Claus and I saw 60 of them wearing maroon instead of red last Saturday. They delivered me the greatest gift I could ask for — A STATE CHAMPIONSHIP TROPHY. I can relax and enjoy Christmas with my wonderful family who sacrificed a husband and dad for the past four months. Thanks again to everyone. Merry Christmas and Happy New Year. May God Bless.

Go Farmers!!!!!

Ronnie

RONNIE GAGE

Lewisville head coach Ronnie Gage has succeeded at what no other Texas High School football coach has been able to accomplish: 5A Division I and Division II titles.

Gage won the Division II title with his 1993 team. It finished the season 15-0-1 and established the record for most victories in a season at Lewisville High School.

Gage did one better in 1996 as his Fighting Farmers finished the season 15-0, the school's first unbeaten, untied season. Since the Farmers battled in the Division I bracket, only 15 games were needed for the Farmers to win a state title.

The Decatur native has been Lewisville's head coach for six years and his teams have qualified for the playoffs each year.

Here is his record:

Lewisville posted a 7-5 record in 1991. Lewisville posted a 10-2-1 record in 1992. The Farmers posted a 15-0-1 record in 1993 and won the Division II state title. The Farmers were 9-4 in 1994, 7-4-1 in 1995 and 15-0 in 1996, another state championship season.

1996, Ronnie's thank-you note to the community after 1996 State Championship win.

out on the field. There was no way I could stand on the sidelines and watch if I couldn't contribute at a high level. Even knowing these things, my passion for coaching still had a lock on me. It made what I had to do so much harder.

Stepping Away from Football

About a week after I got out of the hospital, Stephanie drove me down to the school. I turned in my resignation letter, the superintendent shook my hand, and I told him there was one last thing I needed to do.

The locker room smelled like stale sweat, just like it always did. My kids were standing right in front of me, all of them looking at me with expectant eyes. My throat caught as I tried to speak, and not just from the pneumonia.

I told them the truth as plainly as I could—I had reached a point where physically it was best for my future for me to step back. I had done it a long time and it was a hard decision, but that didn't diminish the expectations I had for them and my gratitude for what they had done for me. The routine of forty-two years was coming to a close. One reason you coach so long is for the love of the kids. I was about to step away from the thing in coaching I loved most. I knew it was the right decision. God guided me through it just the same as He had done throughout my career. I had come to peace with it, but that did not make it any easier.

I talked to them about continuing to do the things they had been doing—working hard, trusting each other, depending on the guy next to them, and to have fun with what they do. Now they had another big-time fan in me, and I would always be there for them if they needed anything. As crushing as it was to tell them that, it felt like the weight of the world was lifted off my shoulders once I did.

Kids are pretty resilient. Some were emotional, some looked

shocked, but most importantly I think they understood and respected my decision and they took it well. They're a good bunch. Just like I'd been blessed with a strong family, I've also been blessed with a strong team. I know they will continue to do great things, and I'll be watching them from the stands.

But we all know I'm going to make my way to the sidelines every chance I get.

Lessons Learned through Unexpected Events

I'm still taking it day by day. When you do something for as long as I coached, life becomes a cycle. I still catch myself thinking, *I should be doing this to prepare for the season*, at certain points during the year. It's hard to sit still most days. I still go to coaching events and talk to old friends. We still talk football, and I'm still involved in the organizations I really care about. It just feels a little different now. Although I don't have a little badge that says "Coach Gage" on my chest anymore, my colleagues always make me feel welcome, which helps this transition so much more.

I've spent a lot of time meditating and thinking about my relationship with God. The most important thing my heart attack has taught me is that the best lesson life teaches us is also the most easily forgotten: This life we have is precious. I learned after Jess passed you can't hug or kiss your loved ones enough. I tell people all the time to take advantage of what you have because tomorrow is not promised.

I loved coaching. It was my greatest passion and I dedicated my life's work to it. As much as I loved it, I now have much more time to spend with my family. Each minute is important, and now I can spend all of them with the people I love. I am looking forward to what comes next.

Faith during Transition

My relationship with God got me through my heart attack, as well as the love and support from family and friends. As much fear as I had, I knew that if it was time to go, I'd approach it as bravely as I could.

I had faith because in those terrifying moments when I realized how little control I had, faith was all I had to hang on to. I knew that if this was it and God had other plans for me, then Jess would be up there waiting for me.

As I was lying in the hospital, when things were still not looking good, I took Stephanie's hand and told her, "If something happens, I want you to approach it with a smile on your face because I want you to envision me up there with our little girl under my arm. She'll have company and everything will be okay." She'd held up so well until that point, as much for me as for herself and our kids, but her eyes watered for a moment. "Not yet," she declared, shaking her head. She'd decided right then and there that I'd make it out of the hospital alive. And once again, she was right.

2016, Touchdown! Still excited after forty-two years of coaching.

I also realized that I could have a better relationship with God. It's so easy to get caught up in the cycle of day to day. I have more time now, and I owe it to God to be a better believer in Him.

HUDDLE UP WITH TOM THOMPSON:
LISTENING TO YOUR HEART

After "the kick" in November of 2009, there was media attention. For a sports news cycle, the headlines read, "61-year-old kicks extra point in college game." The administration at Austin College, Coach Gage, and I expected a fair amount of media attention. That possibility had been discussed when I first started practicing. The last thing Coach Gage wanted to be doing was sitting for interviews with the *New York Times* and CNN.

There were some of those opportunities after the kick. A local CBS affiliate interviewed Coach Gage, and I could tell he was perturbed he had to take time out to speak with them. There was the business of football to be dealt with, and reporters didn't factor in to the game Ronnie Gage liked to play.

Don't Take the Easy Way Out

I had a few decisions of my own to make. The semester was almost over when the football season ended. The entire reason I enrolled for an undergraduate degree and promised to go on to grad school was to play football. No one could take the accomplishment away from me now, even if I didn't enroll in classes the next semester. And it sure would be nice to be back home more and to avoid that drive every day if I didn't have to. So I decided to consult the wisest person I knew, my wife, Teresa.

We were sitting at the kitchen table one morning after the kick, when I asked her point blank, "Okay, are you ready for me to come home now and be a husband and a dad?"

My wife looked at me and said, "You've never quit anything in your life. You are not about to quit now. You've got to show those kids that you didn't go to that school just to play football."

The truth was, I *had* quit before. Multiple times. I'd quit college when I was younger, quit a few marriages, quit jobs, quit my faith, and quit on myself. But I'd also never had such support behind me and around me as I did now.

In addition to that, Teresa had hit on a few points that I had not thought about in my fatigue. I'm not too proud to admit that I was tired. My leg had improved, but I still hurt. Finals were coming up too. My wife, however, cut through all of that and reminded me what my true purpose was. Part of the reason I wanted to play college football was selfish. Suiting up and being on a team was something I wanted to do.

I also wanted to do something to inspire people. Through my karate and other endeavors, I wanted to show people that seemingly unobtainable goals could happen. This wasn't a "people of a certain age" thing. Even though I was older, I didn't want to just inspire people who were knocking at retirement's door. I wanted to help people achieve their goals no matter where they were in their life. How would it look to the kids on campus, or my teammates, if I up and quit school? How would I feel if I slinked away? God had shown me this path for a reason, so I stayed.

Sticking with the Plan, Even through the Pain

The hardest decisions we must make are usually associated with pain and fatigue. We wearily drive up to the crossroads and sometimes don't care what decision we make. The mess can be cleaned up after, but often we're too tired to make a good decision right now. Those are the moments when pausing can be your best play.

Many of life's decisions don't need to be made *on the spot.* Unlike the movies where the hero disarms the ticking time bomb by making a split-second decision, we have the luxury of time. There are a few moments to call a friend or at least pray about which path to take. Don't let the prospect of one more thing force you into a bad decision.

The flip side of taking your time to decide is knowing when you've stayed too long at the party. I don't think anyone would say that Coach Gage was a quitter. There are likely many he's coached throughout the years who would consider those fighting words. But sometimes circumstances dictate that our best course of action is to step away.

You're not a quitter if you stop doing something that is, or will become, detrimental to you. Being able to discern when to quit takes the wisdom of Solomon and the patience of Job, but you'll know the signs. Listen to your heart and the guidance He is giving you. It's there if you allow yourself to see it.

13

A Wife's Perspective

By Stephanie Gage

The first thing I learned about being married to a coach was it's not a private kind of job. Ronnie had a public job and working for a public entity, that means a lot of your personal business is put out there for everybody to view. The good part about that is you become aware that your behavior has bigger consequences. Coaches and their families serve as good role models for a school and community. You must live up to that standard.

1970, Stephanie as senior cheerleader.

The opposite side of the limelight is that people can be mean. You hear everything from hurtful comments in the grocery store to people wrongfully believing our children got special privileges. There's a balance to be had. You must become the momma and papa bear being protective of your child's privacy, while being a good role model.

I Embraced His Career

I understood all of that from the beginning and still embraced Ronnie's career. It was not an easy life. It's not for every spouse out there either. You are a single parent a great amount of the year. There are decisions that have to be made on your own. Unless you can find the inner strength to deal with these tribulations, you are going to be unhappy. If you need a partner around you all the time to make decisions and you can't do anything on your own—then that's certainly not the life for you. However, if you approach the challenges with a passion for overcoming obstacles, being part of a coach's life is something to love. All of that was easier with Ronnie. He's so passionate about coaching, it's hard not to get excited right along with him.

Ronnie was also grounded in the values that mattered most to his family. Many men hide behind the protector and provider roles to duck out of events with the kids. Ronnie was twice as busy

1993, Stephanie on sidelines after playoff game in 1993.

as most men that "just don't have the time" to participate, but he always did find the time, even when we lived nearly an hour away from the school. Leading up to his first state championship in 1993, we hadn't yet moved from Justin. It was forty-five-minute drive between Justin and Lewisville, which added to my and Ronnie's already packed days. But we were both committed and we made it work.

The postseason ran right up to Christmas, and we were still attending a little church in Justin. We were active in the church and that year Juli had the lead role in the play. They needed extras for the musical, so Ronnie and I sang alongside the other cast member from the church. Ronnie participated in that church musical and the month of practices until it was over, even though it was in the middle of the postseason leading up to the state championship. There were so many other commitments, but Ronnie wanted to be there at that little church for our daughter. He didn't miss any of it because his family is the most important thing to him, no matter what was going on at school.

With an example like that, it was easier for me to make the commitments I made to Ronnie with his set of values. I always knew that we were equal partners.

Helping Your Partner through Transition

Forty-two years is a long time to do something. Sports has been with Ronnie his entire life, so it truly has been his lifestyle. I was concerned when he had to step back from sports for his health. When you have loved something as much as he has loved it and have it stripped away unexpectedly, that's a blow some people can never recover from. But thankfully, we've been able to keep busy doing other things so we're not sitting at home feeling sad about things we can't control. It's also given us both the opportunities to participate in hobbies and in organizations we love.

One of the Facebook groups I belong to is the Texas High School Coaches' Wives Association. I love being a mentor to young wives and making sure that they know what they are getting into. There were questions about how to handle young kids at games, how to support your coach during a tough season, and a thousand other things. Each post was a glimpse into their hearts.

It was hard for me to read their posts during the time of Ronnie's health problems. Their posts were full of excitement for the upcoming season, but I wasn't a part of that for the first time in a long time because I was focused on helping Ronnie recover.

I loved being a coaches' wife. I loved working at the schools. I just loved our lifestyle. When that changed suddenly, he wasn't the only one who had to grieve that loss. The transition was going to take some adjustment for the both of us. But we are working on finding our way. We always have.

I was recently talking to someone about how fortunate we are to have two kids who are coaching. Ronnie and I will able to keep a part of our old lives going through our children's efforts. We'll have to be spectators rather than participants right now, but it's different when you're watching your kids.

We plan on being as involved as we can, and maybe that will help with the healing part of what we are leaving behind. That is probably the way it is for anybody who retires from something they love, where there's a loss of the purpose that you had every day coming into work.

We miss that extra bit of the excitement at the start of the season, but I've willingly traded that lifestyle since it means I get to keep my husband. This year, I won't be looking at Ronnie as he stands on the sidelines. Instead I'll be sitting next to him in the stands. Together we'll help each other through the changes as they come.

How Coaching Has Enriched My Life

Being front and center in a community is a place that is never lonely. When Ronnie's teams were successful, and especially when they weren't, a lot of people wanted to talk about the team. From your next-door neighbor to the person behind you at the grocery store, they all want to get the inside story.

That was more prevalent in Lewisville after the 1993 state championship. Ronnie was a minor celebrity after that win. They had never won a state championship before. Bringing hope and pride to the town that had never had notoriety before is powerful.

As Ronnie's family, we were on the bandwagon with that. The state championship opened doors for Ronnie that we had never considered before. There were media interviews and companies who wanted Ronnie to speak at their meetings. Football clinics were suddenly interested in having Ronnie speak too. I always went with him to those events.

I didn't miss Ronnie's games unless Juli had a volleyball game. It was hard for Juli and me, but her games were always a priority. There weren't conflicts for Jess or James, because Jess was a cheerleader and James was either on the sidelines or playing, and they did not miss games. Juli had graduated by the time James played on varsity, so I did not have to choose between which of their games to attend.

I was never one of those mothers who said it was too much trouble to take your child to the game because they had to be in bed at a certain time. A community recognizes that level of dedication in a coach's family. Members of the community recognized the family's dedication and they appreciated what we were giving back to them.

The Community Truly Matters

Out of all the gifts I've received being a coach's wife, becoming an

1991, Fighting Farmer family. Always his biggest supporters.

integral part of different communities has been the greatest. That's translated to why our children have become coaches. Those career choices were made not just because of Ronnie's work ethic but also because Ronnie understands he's more than a coach. Coach Gage is a respected member of the community who enhances the lives of all the residents. He's helped to create small-town heroes and hope where there was little more than dust blowing over the streets.

Our kids loved that feeling of being connected to a town. I think you'll find that with most coach's families. You would think they would resent the hectic life, since a coach is on the go steadily at least four months out of the year and most of the year if he is the athletic director too. That's a lot of time during our children's younger years where Ronnie was tending to other people's children. Our children saw little of him during those months but still came back to coaching themselves. You'd be surprised at how many coaches' kids become coaches themselves.

I think the coaches' kids become coaches because of their love of the sport. They are made for this career because they have learned innate flexibility and socialization from their life growing up as a coach's kid. Coaches' kids meet a lot of different types of people and are usually social. Their best friends are often other coaches' kids because everyone spends most of their time supporting the team in one way or another. As they say, it takes a village. You find that in the coaching community, everybody lends a hand with everybody's kids. That is just the way that it works and probably couldn't work any other way.

Nobody understands that lifestyle more than other coaches' wives and families. Our kids loved Ronnie coaching and the lifestyle coaching brought with it. They never, ever were upset about his time away. They were proud of him for the difference he was making.

To make a difference in the community and to have that group embrace you—how could I have ever wanted anything more out of this life? Being a nurse, I knew I'd be caring for individuals. I didn't understand how I'd be caring for an entire community. And I didn't understand how much the community would care for me and my children back. That's a blessing I wouldn't trade for the world.

HUDDLE UP WITH TOM THOMPSON:
IT TAKES A VILLAGE TO MAKE A VILLAGE

The gifts Stephanie gained weren't directly from the football field. The concepts of community and personal growth were a result of Ronnie's coaching, but many of the lessons she learned were through her own experiences in being a Christian, a nurse, a wife, a mom, and a constant encourager.

Honestly, I've learned a gazillion spiritual lessons, but they haven't all been directly tied to the football community. While my entire life has circled around football, many of the lessons I've learned have been a direct result of trying to get back on the field, over almost forty years of life experience. The lessons are learned during the journey and not necessarily once you reach the endpoint.

The journey encompasses faith-building and understanding how to be faithfully patient. We talk about being faithful and being patient as if they are separate items. One has to combine the two to make any long-term or difficult goal work. Those *almost out of reach goals* I choose will hopefully inspire other people to do the great things God has in store for them.

I have no intention for anyone to replicate what I've done, because everybody has their own story. Having the willingness to be courageous enough to live the chapters of our own story requires faithful patience and inspiration. God is constantly speaking to us, but we have to be willing to hear.

Being Your Best Self

When God speaks to us about achieving goals within a team or organization, there are some ground rules that are easy to forget. If you are not at 100 percent, then there is no way you can give 100 percent to anything. "The best you" puts you in a position to help the team or the organization be the best at what they are doing.

At work, if you show up but are not prepared and excited, that affects organizational performance. Your performance individually can be linked to the overall performance of the organization. Performance in a group isn't a contest. You are not tasked with being better than anybody else. You should help others see the best in themselves.

Isn't that exactly what Stephanie found out by being an example for each community where Ronnie was coaching? She sacrificed her time to become involved not only in Ronnie's coaching but also for the good of her neighbors by exhibiting self-leadership. How can you lead others when you can't lead yourself? You must learn to lead yourself first.

I find that the easiest way to exhibit self-leadership is to put myself on an established routine that is proven to give results. That includes the basics of proper sleep, balanced diet, and scheduled workouts. Do those whether you feel like it or not, and eventually you'll realize how much better you feel and function when you have a consistent daily routine.

I knew if I didn't do those key points, I was not going to have any shot at being on a football field. If it was raining and I was scheduled to run, I would run on the treadmill. You find ways to work toward your goals, no matter the obstacles. That's what leaders do for their followers and exactly what one does when exhibiting self-leadership—you are faithfully patient on the journey to your goals.

Ronnie and Stephanie came to that same conclusion early in their careers. If they had not, I doubt Ronnie would have impacted the lives of the students he has over the last forty-two years. Forget the state championships—the impact on thousands of people's lives is Ronnie Gage's crowning achievement.

14

Semi-Retired

The hardest aspect of leaving my profession isn't leaving behind a routine. One would think that there would be a rhythm to a forty-two-year career. There was, if one looks to school years, football seasons, and summer vacations. That's where the routine ended.

What I will probably miss is the constant change. While some people dread change, I thrived with it. There was always a new group of kids every year; how they interacted and formed a team was new. There were always new training methods to evaluate and ways to inspire the team. There was so much new happening in my coaching world, that new became routine.

Adjusting to a low-key life—that will be a challenge. I do piddle a lot now. I do my own yard work and catch up on honey-dos. Someone asked me what do you do now with your spare time? I thought a minute and said, "You know, I don't know," but it seems I'm never at home and I don't get bored. I have made enough contacts over the years that if I want to work, I can sell turf or sporting goods. That is not something I really want to do though. I want to focus instead on what's important.

I have a cabin on a lake and grandkids. I've never had the extended time to spend much time at the lake with them, and I'm

2019, April 2019, Gage Family

looking forward to making new memories. I've already started the process of chasing them around more often at the request of my children. It seems that most phone calls from my own kids these days start with, "Uhh . . . Dad would you mind . . . " And that's fine with me. Being a coach (and grandfather) is about being of service to others. I'll step in and help when and wherever I can. Coach and Pokey will always be available for our precious kids and grandkids.

Unexpected Blessings

You hear about couples who retire and realize they don't like each other anymore. They were so busy at the business of marriage and careers and raising kids that they forgot how to be a married couple.

I was a little worried about Stephanie and me spending so much time together. She retired three years ago when we came back to Decatur from South Texas. That gave her time to volunteer and mentor others and do whatever she wanted to do. So I wondered if she'd want to spend time with me, or if she'd gotten used to doing her own thing without me.

I'm happy to report we have already spent more time together this past year than we have in the last forty-two years it seems, and it's been great. We are both active and we like to do things together. We have plans to do a little traveling and spend some time being in each other's space.

HEY COACH,

OUR SENIOR PASTOR GAVE US THESE CARDS AND ENCOURAGED US TO REACH OUT TO SOMEONE IN OUR LIVES THAT REALLY MADE A DIFFERENCE. I THOUGHT OF YOU. I STILL THINK OF YOU WHEN THE GOING GETS TOUGH AND AM REMINDED TO NEVER GIVE UP. I'M COACHING MY OWN KIDS NOW IN SOCCER, BASKETBALL, AND T-BALL. I HOPE YOUR DOING WELL. LOVE, RYAN LOCKHART

2019, One of many thank-you notes that Ronnie has received from ex-players over the years.

Stephanie and I have a loving marriage and always have. I'm looking forward to the future we create together.

Looking Back over a Legacy

One of the favorite questions people always want to ask a coach at the end of his career is if I've had any regrets. I truly don't have any. I'd start over tomorrow and do the same things. Have I made mistakes along the way? Of course, I have. Haven't you? There's always that person who is happy to bring up a choice you made on the field thirty years ago that didn't turn out so great. I wish that type of person well.

I'd heard once that there's a difference between climate and weather. The weather for a few days might be cold and rainy. That doesn't mean the rest of the year isn't sunny and seventy-five. The sunny and seventy-five is the climate. It's easier sometimes to remember the few rainy days and forget your climate. I think my professional climate has been a good one and that's the legacy I hope to leave behind. I will always cherish the title of "Coach," and I hope the capsule of my life will be remembered as one of purpose for the good.

HUDDLE UP WITH TOM THOMPSON:
COACH'S LEGACY OF LOVE

You might think that a rough and tumble football coach having a legacy of love is an oil-and-water concept. For some coaches, love has no place on their field. For Ronnie Gage, he wouldn't get out of bed in the morning if it wasn't for love. He loves his players. He loves his assistant coaches. He loves his peers. He loves his family. He loves God. Ronnie Gage demonstrates love in everything he does, and it is real. There is no trick he picked up in a coaching clinic or leadership conference. Ronnie Gage is the real deal.

Loving doesn't mean that you give someone a pass for poor performance. Ronnie holds himself accountable. He holds the players and his staff accountable. Coach Gage doesn't hold his charges accountable for outcomes; instead he holds everyone accountable for the process of preparation. You might never set foot on the playing field, but you practice like the next game is the Super Bowl.

If you played for Coach Gage, you knew you were accountable

for the process of being part of a team. Once you understood that and were part of his team, you were always a teammate to Ronnie. That's why so many kids have gone into coaching because of him.

A Teammate and Friend

I remained a teammate for Coach Gage long after our professional association ended. When I was there at Austin College, Coach Gage would sometimes set me up a practice kick. Often, he'd say, "I bet you a Diet Coke you're not going to make it."

Coach Gage got the better end of that deal when I started to make the bets double or nothing. I ended up owing him a few cases and repaid my debt by dropping the cases off on his office desk. Once I even had a case delivered to his house.

The mutual respect between Coach Gage and his players goes far beyond practice bets and good times. When Ronnie was going through all kinds of horrors with his daughter Jess's illness, one of our football players collapsed and died while he was playing a pick-up game of basketball with some teammates. We later learned he had a congenital heart defect that had gone undiagnosed. He'd been playing for years with a ticking time bomb in his chest. It was an absolute tragedy to lose this bright young man, especially in such an unexpected way—a player in his prime, a loving son, friend, and teammate.

Soon after the ambulance took the young man away, Coach Gage was notified. He had a very good excuse to stay where he was, which was at Jess's bedside. After all, his daughter was terminally ill. Still, Ronnie came to Austin College to address the team in one of the most compassionate and faithful messages I've ever witnessed. How could a man whose daughter was dying, and who had just lost a young player, stand up in front of the team and speak about the goodness of God? Because he had a deep faith in God. I've never heard anyone—even a pastor—speak in such a moving way. It was a very powerful message, and one that was greatly needed in that very moment. After the emotional meeting, Ronnie got in his truck and drove back to be with his daughter.

There were many times I'd find him weeping uncontrollably in his truck before practices, and then he'd go to work and coach his heart out all day. As soon as the day was done, he'd drive back to be at his daughter's bedside each night. As far as I know, most of the players didn't know anything about Jess being sick. In fact, upon learning that she'd passed, countless players reacted in shock by saying they hadn't known she was ill to begin with. I suspect Coach Gage didn't want to tell his players because he didn't want them to worry about something that was beyond their control. In the end, Jess's illness was something even the doctors couldn't control. Yet, he continued to operate with faith and love, even in the depths of pain.

Love is all around Ronnie Gage, and you don't have to look far to find it.

Old-School and All Heart

Coach Gage is an old-school tough type of coach. Yet when you look into his eyes, there's a sparkle that gives you the sense he loves you. There is no separation between love and coaching. He was taught by coaches that loved him and that's how he coaches.

In the coaching profession these days, love isn't seen much. Metrics and statistics have been substituted for heart-to-heart talks. That type of coaching might create an athlete who can perform in the spotlight, but coaching the way Ronnie Gage does it creates better men all around.

I am proud of the fact that I can call Coach Gage my coach. I am privileged to be able to call him my friend.

God has blessed me beyond measure. I was once that eager kid who wanted to play college football. I didn't get to play when I thought the time was right. Instead, I got to play college football when He wanted me to.

I'd like to think that He wanted me to meet Ronnie Gage.

A Coach

A coach is like a teacher, teaching many skills,
Not only about the game you play, but about the way life is.

A coach is like a friend, he's there right by your side,
In good times and in bad times, in times you laugh or cry.

A coach is like a counselor, he listens everyday,
He helps you with your problems, he knows the words to
say.

A coach is like a doctor, he has to find what's wrong,
He has to make it better so the team can move along.

A coach will help you deal with loss and teach you how to
win.
He'll take the team that once was boys and turn them into
Men.

ABOUT THE AUTHORS

Ronnie Gage was raised in Decatur, Texas, and developed a love of sports as a young boy. After the death of his father, at the age of thirteen, he looked up to his coaches as role models and decided to become a coach as his vocation. Ronnie started as a middle school coach in 1976 and worked his way up the coaching ladder until he was hired for his first head job in 1987. In 1993, he led the Lewisville High School Fighting Farmers to their first state football championship and repeated it again in 1996.

He recently retired after forty-two years of coaching Texas high school football and molding the lives of thousands of students throughout the years. His love of the profession led him to become an active member of the Texas High School Coaches' Association, and he served as the president of the state-wide organization of 18,000 members in 2004–05. In 2009, he received the ultimate recognition of high school coaches in Texas by being inducted in the THSCA Hall of Honor.

Over the years, Ronnie has coached in five different school districts in Texas and has returned to live in his hometown of Decatur, Texas, with his wife of forty-two years, Stephanie. They are the parents of three children, Jessica, Julianne, and James. Two children followed in his footsteps by becoming coaches. Julianne Penix currently coaches track and volleyball, and his son James is a football coach. He has three grandchildren who are the "light of his life." Ronnie and Stephanie spend as much free time as possible following their children as they coach, playing with grandkids, and watching college football games and the Dallas Cowboys.

Dr. Emmet C. (Tom) Thompson II kicked his way into the record books on November 14, 2009. At age 61, he became the oldest football player in NCAA history and the oldest NCAA football player to score a point when he kicked the PAT (point after touchdown) in the second quarter of the game between Austin College and Trinity University. It was a dream come true—many years in the making.

Like many people, Tom grew up feeling as though he couldn't catch a break. With obstacles and setbacks from a very early age, he struggled to find meaning and purpose. As an adult with no real plan, his self-absorbed lifestyle led to divorce, financial stress, and physical injuries. But in time, he found his faith, his purpose, and his soulmate. If his story says anything, it is that it is never too late to re-imagine what you want your life to be.

With degrees in business management, kinesiology, strategic leadership, and teaching, Dr. Thompson's purpose is to encourage people of all ages to live healthy and fulfilled lives, to discover and reach their full potential, and to develop a deeper faith in the process.

Alice Sullivan is a ghostwriter, *New York Times* bestselling editor (11 times over), author coach, and speaker. A natural-born storyteller, she's written 38 books and edited over 1,300 titles since 2001. In addition to the NYT bestsellers, other books have achieved Amazon bestseller status and won several awards, such as Readers' Choice, Living Now Book Award, and Nashville's Best Local Children's Book Award.

Some of her more notable clients include Jen Hatmaker, Dave Ramsey, Donald Miller, Michael Hyatt, Mastin Kipp, Danette May, Shaquille O'Neal, Manny Pacquiao, George Foreman III, Lee Greenwood, Thomas Steinbeck, Pam Tillis, Bill Cosby, Tony Jeary,

Bill Bennett, and Judge Andrew Napolitano. She's written books for Forbes, Hay House, Thomas Nelson Publishers (now Harper Collins), Made for Grace Publishing, World Net Daily, Changing Lives Press, Clovercroft, and Carpenters Son Publishing.

Alice specializes in memoir, business leadership, and personal growth. She helps her clients identify their goals and messages, creating engaging content to connect with their target markets. Her favorite projects are those that challenge her point of view, expand her knowledge, introduce her to inspiring authors, and add meaning to her life.

Coaching from the Heart

Creating a Legacy of Leadership
from the Sidelines through a Lifetime

Coach Ronnie Gage, M.Ed.
and Emmet C. (Tom) Thompson II, D.S.L.
with Alice Sullivan

Legendary Texas football coach Ronnie Gage teams up with business leadership expert Tom Thompson in a heartfelt and hard-hitting playbook about the profession of coaching. Gage and Thompson provide proven coaching outcomes for all sports—not just football. Readers will be pleasantly surprised to learn that these same lessons also apply to senior management across any organization. Coaching is about far more than team building, huddles, running plays, and lockerroom speeches. It's about seeing the best in others, setting realistic expectations, encouraging them to peak performance, and celebrating each win along the way—whether on the field or in the boardroom. *Coaching from the Heart* is about serving others with love, and teaching lessons that will sustain success over a lifetime.